Building

The

Client

Bond

Series

FROM AAHA PRESS

The Practical Guide To Client Grief

Support Techniques for
15 Common Situations

by Laurel Lagoni, MS

press

First published in the USA by AAHA Press, a division of the
American Animal Hospital Association
12575 West Bayaud Avenue
Lakewood, Colorado 80228

ISBN 0-941451-60-7

This book was designed and produced by
AAHA Press
PO Box 150899
Denver, Colorado 80215

Consultants
Gary Bishop
Suicide Resource Center of Larimer County Colorado

Dr. Merry Crimi

Carolyn Butler, MS

Suzanne Hetts, PhD

Design and Typography
Erin K. Small

Cover Design and Illustration
Dave Bonick

Acknowledgments

No book comes about in isolation. For this book to come to fruition, two women in particular played important roles. I would like to thank Debby Morehead, the American Animal Hospital Association's (AAHA's) savvy acquisitions editor, for her original idea, guidance, enthusiasm, business acumen, and, most of all, her friendship. While writing this book has been rewarding, the greatest personal rewards have come from getting to know Debby as a friend and colleague.

Also deserving of credit is Judy Mazarin, AAHA's publications coordinator. Judy lent her editorial wisdom to this project and shepherded it to completion. She was patient with my conceptual changes and supportive of the final book. Without her, I may not have found such a satisfying way to have a voice in veterinary medicine even after my resignation from the Changes program at Colorado State University. I appreciate all of the doors she has opened for me.

I also want to express my gratitude to the veterinarians, animal health technicians, AAHA readers, and other colleagues who contributed to the revision and production phases of this project. Your insights and comments were invaluable, and the content and scope of this project is more realistic and usable because of them. Gail Bishop of the Suicide Resource Center of Larimer County deserves a special thanks for facilitating the review of the helping strategy concerning suicide. Dr. Merry Crimi wrote a wonderful foreword and deserves special recognition. My personal gratitude is extended to W.B. Saunders Co. and to Carolyn Butler, MS, and Suzanne Hetts, PhD, my co-authors on *The Human-Animal Bond and Grief*. Without their clinical innovations and professional collaboration, many of the concepts in this book would not exist.

Dedications

This series is dedicated to my friends and colleagues at both Colorado State University and the American Animal Hospital Association. Their joint efforts and financial support saved Changes: The Support for People and Pets Program in 1989 when it was in danger of being terminated due to a lack of funds. Thank you all for believing that grieving for companion animals is worthy of our collective emotional, intellectual, financial, and professional investments.

I would also like to dedicate this book to my own companion animals who died in 1996: Casey, our curmudgeon tomcat, and Tai, our sweet, old golden retriever.

Contents

Client Support Concepts:
What You Need to Know

Client Support Strategies:
How to Help in 15 Common Situations

Client Support Resources:
Tools For You to Use

Figures

Meet the Author **68**

Foreword

Some of life's toughest assignments are the ones for which we get the least preparation. And so it is with the sudden accidental loss or euthanasia of our clients' companions and the delicate process we try to guide them through to find peace and a sense of closure, just when they find it most difficult to ask for our help.

If you and your staff are like many, you may have never really learned any formal etiquette surrounding euthanasia or pet loss. You probably decided to model euthanasia in a way that you'd like it to be handled for your own pets. Unfortunately, not all clients think like we do. Not all of them want the same options we'd want. And often, when their wishes differ from what ours might be, we're uncomfortable with what other alternatives might look and feel like. Sometimes their reactions during and after a loss differ profoundly from what we're expecting or what we've made time for.

In *The Practical Guide to Client Grief*, Laurel Lagoni gives our profession a tool we've been long awaiting. Something we can read now for general use during times of client grief, as well as save for a ready reference for unique and difficult situations. It makes an exquisite teaching tool and provides significant points worthy of group discussion for the entire health care team. The use of this reference will define for us the opportunities and provide the skills to dialogue with our staff members on issues that stress them the most— issues that they seldom get the opportunity to verbalize. Laurel defines and legitimizes the help we offer in supporting our valued clients through the toughest decisions they face with their pets. She provides specific actions for some of the toughest communications challenges we have in veterinary practice.

I hope that you'll use this book to tailor your hospital's euthanasia protocols and to educate your health care team on the importance of handling clients in the most supportive manner possible when they look to veterinary professionals for the answers and options they need to get through difficult times. In turn, I know you'll see, in the faces of your clients, reflections of the sensitivity, understanding, and dignity you've invested in them as the keepers of those who cannot speak or make decisions for themselves.

Dr. Merry Crimi, Hospital Director,
Gladstone Veterinary Clinic
1996–1997 AAHA President

Preface

Welcome to the human side of veterinary medicine! You may not have been told that veterinary medicine is a helping profession. A helping profession is one, such as nursing or counseling, that provides direct services to people to fulfill one or more of their needs. On a daily basis, you treat valuable members of peoples' families (their ill or injured companion animals). Thus, you do meet one of their most important needs and provide a vital human service.

During medical crises and companion animal deaths, you often need to help your human clients as well as treat their animal patients. Yet, you probably haven't received a great deal of training in this area. A survey conducted by Drs. Fogle and Abrahamson reports on this deficiency in training. Fogle and Abrahamson report that, of the veterinarians they surveyed, 96 percent had received no training on how to explain terminal illness to clients, and 72 percent felt this training would be helpful.[1] This book was written to provide you with some simple, basic information about how to provide support to your human clients, especially during times of grief.

The information in this book is based primarily on the knowledge and skills gleaned through Changes: The Support for People and Pets Program at the Colorado State University Veterinary Teaching Hospital. The Changes program was created in 1984 and today is the most comprehensive, on-site veterinary grief support program in the world. When the Changes program began, little was known about what would and would not be helpful to the grieving pet owners who brought their beloved companion animals to the teaching hospital. Staff members were unsure about how to handle grief, client anger, or the stress of the veterinary medical professionals with whom they worked. However, as new techniques and client support strategies were applied to research findings about loss and grief, certain issues, concerns, and responses emerged as being more helpful than others. Chief among these helpful interventions was a method of conducting euthanasia which allowed, and even encouraged, pet owners to be present with their pets when veterinarians helped companion animals die. This method is called ceremonial owner-present euthanasia. Today, it serves as the foundation of the Changes program.

All pet owners who truly love their cats, dogs, horses, birds, rabbits, or other animals deserve the opportunity to say good-bye to their pets in positive, meaningful ways. It is the responsibility of all veterinary professionals to ensure that their clients have these opportunities. You can accomplish this by learning about the normal symptoms of grief, by learning how to help pet owners cope with grief, and by learning how to conduct client-present euthanasias in sensitive, compassionate ways.

The goal for this book is to provide you with easily applied, easily understood information about what to say and what to do in a variety of grief-related situations. This book isn't filled with a lot of theory, detailed background information, or textbook methodologies. Instead, this book is filled with phrases and actions designed to give you quick, easy access to effective client support strategies.

There are very few right or wrong answers or techniques when it comes to providing client support. A strategy that works well for one person may not work as well for another. However, there are client support strategies that, in general, are the most effective ones to use with the majority of pet owners and situations you will encounter during your professional life.

Of course, there is much more to be learned about the human-animal bond, communication, stress, and helping pet owners deal with grief. The following information represents only the essential knowledge and skills you need. If you wish to read more about these topics, several books are recommended in the Resources section.

Client Support Concepts

What You Need to Know

Who is This Book For?

This book is intended for use both as a personal reference and as a model for staff development. It is designed to help you and your co-workers handle many of the grief-related situations you encounter on a day-to-day basis while on the job in veterinary medicine.

Each member of your veterinary staff, including **veterinarians**, **veterinary technicians**, **office managers**, and **receptionists**, will learn to:
- Increase your personal knowledge about the effects of companion animal death
- Improve your client support skills
- Deal with your grief during patient deaths

In addition,
- As a **veterinarian**, you can provide your staff with the information and skills they need to provide client support.
- As a **veterinary technician**, you can enhance your professional growth.
- As an **office manager**, you can provide your staff with the training and skills they need to provide client support and improve staff and client retention.
- As a **receptionist**, you can learn new ways to deal with difficult emotional situations, making them less stressful for staff and clients.

How to Use this Book

There are three ways to use this book:

As a Preparatory Study Guide
This method encourages you to anticipate the issues and circumstances of your upcoming cases and to read about some of the words and techniques you might try when you're face-to-face with pet owners. This method works best when you have warning about the issues that may arise, such as in cases that involve euthanasia or that involve children who must deal with companion animal death.

As an On-the-spot Assistance Guide
This method encourages you to realize when you are in a situation where you have no idea what to say or what to do, and to excuse yourself for a few minutes while you consult this book for helping strategies. After arming yourself with appropriate techniques, you can go back to your clients and ease their emotions, tension, or grief.

As a Professional Growth or Teaching Tool
This method encourages you to process the cases you have just been involved with by analyzing what you did well and what you might have done better. This learning process can take place on your own as you read about the situations you were involved with and the suggestions about how they could be handled. The learning process can also be used as a case study for debriefing during staff meetings.

Debriefing involves talking openly with your co-workers about the emotional, as well as the medical, aspects of your cases and receiving feedback and support for the helping actions you took. When you participate in a debriefing session, you present the emotional as well as the medical elements of your case, describe what the emotional dilemmas were for you and the pet owner, and talk about the helping strategies you tried. In other words:
- Explain what you felt went well. ("This technique really worked!")
- Explain what you felt didn't go well. ("Mrs. James seemed to get angry with me when I suggested she might want to include her son in her decision-making efforts.")
- Ask your colleagues for ideas about other ways to handle the situation. ("How do the rest of you deal with suggestions that seem to offend clients?")

Some special features are included in this book. They are designed to help you become a more effective communicator and source of support during grief and times of stress. For example, each Client Support Strategy has a notes area for you to record your thoughts on what worked and what didn't work in each situation. Recording and occasionally reviewing your notes will help you develop your own vocabulary, helping style, and customized guide to helping clients deal with grief. Write down the phrases, gestures, ideas, and methods your clients seem to respond to in a positive way, so you can be sure to repeat them next time you face that same situation.

There also is a feedback form on page 63 which you can use as a discussion tool during debriefing sessions and staff meetings. The best way to use this form is to make multiple copies and have it available for staff members' use. Also develop a way that you and your co-workers can receive feedback confidentially.

Finally, there is a list of references and resources for those of you who would like to read more about these topics. In addition, there is a glossary for easy reference, so you can have ready access to supportive language.

The Human Side of Veterinary Medicine

Five years ago, a golden retriever named Roxy, a beloved member of the Murphy family, died during risky surgery. The veterinarian called the family immediately to deliver the sad news. An hour later, Gail Murphy called us.

"They insist on seeing it!" Gail said in an anxious voice. "I can't believe it would be good for them to see it!" she cried. "They" were her two sons, 6-year-old Randy and 9-year-old Jeff. "It" was Roxy's body. When told of Roxy's death, Gail's children had followed their instincts and asked to see their pet. Like any parent, Gail was caught between wanting to honor her children's wishes and protecting them from further trauma.

As Carolyn talked with Gail, she praised her desire to be a responsible parent, but explained that Western society is uncomfortable with death and unsure about how to heal from loss. Carolyn reassured Gail that it was normal and emotionally healthy for her sons to want to see their dog's body and she encouraged her to allow her sons to say a proper good-bye to their best friend. "It will be painful to view Roxy's body," Carolyn said, "but it might be more painful later for Randy and Jeff if you don't allow them to see Roxy's body. They may feel like they abandoned her." Still hesitant, Gail agreed.

Several hours later, the Murphy family gathered in our counseling office. Gail sat on the couch, her husband, Brian, perched awkwardly on the arm of a chair, and the boys hovered in the doorway, anxious to be taken to Roxy. Laurel explained that Roxy's body had been brought into the exam room next door, where she was now lying on a large, soft pad on the floor. In preparation for viewing Roxy's body, Laurel provided the Murphys with details about what they would see and feel should they choose to remove the blanket that covered Roxy's body. "Her eyes are still open and, if you want to hug her, she may feel a bit stiff," she concluded. "Her face and head are uncovered and Roxy still looks like Roxy."

"If you're ready now, I'll take you to Roxy," Carolyn said. The boys nodded, but the parents elected to wait in our office.

Carolyn led Randy and Jeff next door. A slender, vertical window, allowed the boys to peek inside. For a few seconds, neither made a move to go in. Then, using his small hand to turn the doorknob, Randy took a deep breath and stepped inside. The door closed behind him and Jeff watched through the window as his younger brother moved slowly toward their dog, carefully pulled down the blanket, and reached out to tentatively stroke the shaved skin below Roxy's incision. As Randy became more comfortable, he touched Roxy's face and even planted a small kiss on the tip of her nose. Then, returning to the exam room door, he opened it and whispered, "She's cold, like when she comes in from the snow …" Inspired by his younger brother's courage, Jeff joined Randy in the exam room, petting Roxy and examining her stitches.

After a few moments, the boys looked up and saw their mother's face at the window. Without a word, Jeff crossed the room, opened the door, and reached out to take his mother's hand. Soon, she was at Roxy's side, crying, apologizing, and thanking the dog for her years of loyal friendship.

Eventually, Brian also said good-bye, embarrassed, as many men are, by his tears and inability to suppress his grief. In a follow-up phone call, it was Brian who captured the healing dimension of the experience, saying, "In our culture, death and grief are taboo subjects. When we talk about them, we sound morose and weak and, let's face it, most people simply don't want to be around that. But this experience was different," he continued, "it made me feel stronger, more able to face difficult situations. I want to tell others to lean into their grief, to let themselves feel all of the pain and despair that is inside of them because, once they have, they will actually begin to feel better. Roxy and my sons taught me that."

Carolyn Butler, MS, and Laurel Lagoni, MS
Reprinted with permission from Dog & Kennel Magazine.

The Human-Animal Bond

Most of society, and even veterinary medicine, hasn't acknowledged it, but the death of a companion animal may be one of the most significant losses we experience in our lives. Why? Let's look at the facts.

Today, more people share their lives with companion animals than with children.[2] This may be because there are more single, divorced, childless, widowed, and elderly people living alone than ever before in the history of Western society. Over the past three decades, the relationships between humans and their companion animals have changed dramatically. In our society, we tend to move a lot. We often choose to live hundreds of miles away from our close relatives and friends. Therefore, pets, even more than other people, have become the constant presence in many of our lives. They have moved into the roles traditionally reserved for other humans. These are the roles of parent, brother, sister, child, confidante, and best friend. Some pet owners even describe their animal friends as soul mates. Surveys and clinical experience tell us that people can readily identify the many benefits of pet ownership. People often include companionship, acceptance, emotional support, and unconditional love among companion animals' most significant and pleasing character traits.[3]

There is also mounting scientific evidence that pets are good for humans, helping to maintain their owners' physical health and psychological well-being. For example, pets have been shown to reduce high stress levels by lowering human heart rate and blood pressure.[4] They have also been known to aid in the recoveries of heart attack survivors and to act as positive agents for people undergoing various types of medical, psychological, and physical therapy treatments.[5]

If you are familiar with animal lore, you know the media frequently reports on companion animals who heroically save their owners' lives. The popular media also feature animals who, more quietly but just as heroically, serve on a day-to-day basis as service animals or guides, becoming their owners' eyes, ears, and even hands. These emotional and heartwarming stories have one thing in common—they are testimonials to the power of the human-animal bond.

The term human-animal bond has become a popular way of referring to the types of relationships and attachments people form with animals, particularly companion animals like dogs, cats, birds, horses, goats, rabbits, snakes, ferrets, and guinea pigs. Bonding with an animal means making a commitment, taking responsibility for it, and letting the animal influence and impact your attitudes, behaviors, decisions, and plans. Bonding implies that an emotional attachment to an animal occurs, that you let yourself feel genuine affection and even love for an animal. This bond can be immensely rewarding as long as the relationship continues. But, when the bond is broken by the animal's death, it can exact a high price.

When the Bond is Broken

According to researchers at the University of California-Davis, veterinary professionals tend to underestimate the importance of the bonds between their clients and patients.[6] Trivializing and negating the significance of the human-animal bond is potentially damaging to the veterinary professional-client relationship. Thus, it is vitally important for veterinary professionals to learn how to attend to companion animal death with compassion. One of the most effective ways to do this is by learning all you can about the experiences of loss and normal grief.

It is difficult to ignore the mounting evidence indicating that the grief people feel at the deaths of their pets is real. Recent studies show that the grief pet owners feel when companion animals die is often overwhelming. Pet owners' responses to pet loss are often as emotional as the grief responses accompanying the loss of a human friend or family member. In one study, 75 percent of pet owners said they experienced disruptions in their lives after their pets died. One third of these pet owners said they experienced difficulties in their relationships with others and/or needed to take time off from work due to their feelings of grief.[7]

Companion animal death is an inevitable part of pet ownership. Pets have relatively short life spans; few pets outlive their owners. Some animals die from illnesses, and others are victims of accidents. Many pets die of old age or are euthanized due to unresolvable behavior problems.

Companion animal death is also an inevitable part of veterinary medicine. In fact, it is estimated that veterinary professionals experience the deaths of their patients five times more often than physicians in human medicine.[8] Of course, euthanasia plays a huge role in creating this statistic. One study looked at animals who are treated and who subsequently die over a period of one year. Sixty-six percent of these deaths are due to euthanasia.

Loss and Grief

As you begin to play a more active role in your clients' experiences with companion animal death, you will find that most people know very little about coping with grief. You will also find that what they do know, or think they know, is generally inaccurate.

Research suggests that what people say and do during bereavement is based on the myths and misinformation about grief that are passed along in families from generation to generation.[10] One of the most damaging of these myths is the belief that the right way to handle loss is to be strong and stoic, never allowing grief to show. Another damaging belief is that staying busy and keeping one's mind off thoughts of loss is the right way to quickly feel better and eventually recover. To avoid reinforcing damaging myths and misinformation, you need to become knowledgeable about the normal, healthy grieving process.

Loss and grief are two of our most common human experiences. However, they are probably the two life experiences about which we know the least. Until recently, conversations about loss, death, and grief have been taboo and viewed as morbid or morose. Yet, in the last three decades, experts have learned a great deal about loss and grief.

Loss is defined as an ending or as a point of change or transition. Grief is defined as the natural and spontaneous response to loss. Grief is the normal way to adjust to endings and changes and is a necessary process for healing emotional wounds. Grief is a process, not an event. It takes a long time to grieve a significant loss. There is no specific time frame in which the grieving process is completed. In fact, normal grief may last for days, weeks, months, or even years, depending on the significance of the loss. If progressing in a healthy manner, grief lessens in intensity over time.

Everyone has a unique response to loss; there is no right or wrong way to grieve. Grief also differs according to peoples' ages, genders, and cultures. For instance, research conclusively confirms that women cry more often during grief than men.[11]

If grief is progressing normally, it follows a fairly predictable course, with an initial, acute phase of shock, despair, or denial, one or more middle phases of emotional pain and suffering, and a final phase of recovery. It is of more use for you to have a basic, working knowledge of the normal symptoms of grief than to have a great deal of theoretical knowledge about how grief progresses. You are more likely to see your clients' grief when it is in the early, acute phases (e.g., during a medical emergency or immediately following a euthanasia) rather than in the middle or final stages.

Pet Owners' Needs and Expectations During Grief

Many pet owners are emotional about their companion animals. In practice, you often witness the love and devotion that exists between pet owners and their pets. When medical problems arise, you also see

their fears and anxieties. When your clients are emotionally distressed, you may want to reach out to them, but you may also feel unsure about how to help them appropriately.

When people are in the midst of emotional crises, it is hard to know what to say or do that will comfort, rather than offend, them. This feeling of helplessness is documented in one research study that reports that 80 percent of the women and 74 percent of the men surveyed said they felt sympathetic and would like to respond in a supportive manner when someone else cries. Yet, the majority of survey participants said they typically don't respond because they don't know what to say or what to do.[12]

Clinical experience shows that when emotions and behaviors associated with grief, like sadness and crying, are repressed, it takes longer to heal from loss. When grief is freely expressed, though, the healing time can be greatly reduced. As a veterinary professional, you can help pet owners heal by encouraging them to talk openly about their grief-related thoughts and feelings. You can also give a client permission to grieve by letting him or her know you understand the need to cry, to ask questions, to be present at the pet's euthanasia, to view the companion animal's body after death, and to reminisce about the pet's life.

Learning to help with strategies like giving permission is important because today's pet owners want more than medical care from you. In fact, studies examining patient satisfaction with human medicine report that caring is a more valuable component of their doctor/patient relationship than curing.[13] Clinical experience has shown that the same attitude prevails in veterinary medicine.

Surveys also find that, along with patients' long-standing wishes for courtesy, respect, sincerity, and honesty, they also want veterinary professionals to acknowledge their emotions and truly listen to their concerns.[14] In other words, pet owners want you to be a competent veterinary professional and a sensitive listener. They want to know you are committed to helping them and that you will stick it out with them, even when the going gets rough. In short, they want to trust you.

According to marketing studies, pet owners do trust veterinarians in a special way. In fact, they most often compare the trust they place in veterinarians to the trust they place in their children's pediatricians.[15] Like pediatricians, veterinarians are viewed by pet owners as caring for the most vulnerable members of their families—those who can not speak or make decisions for themselves.

Pet owners also see veterinarians as authority figures. Therefore, even though they are often intimidated by veterinarians, they also depend on veterinarians and veterinary staff for guidance and emotional reassurance. Your role is an influential one, and this influence makes clients' expectations of you extremely high.

When clients' feelings are not acknowledged with sincerity and respect, many become dissatisfied, disillusioned, and even angry. In fact, the results of one survey showed that 68 percent of survey participants stopped going to a veterinary practice due to the indifferent attitudes of one or more of its employees.[16]

Even when there is no longer anything you can do medically to help your animal patients, there is still a great deal you can do emotionally to help your human clients. When your helping philosophy includes this thought, you will realize that patient death is not the worst that can happen. Rather, the worst that can happen is that a pet owner you don't help will fail to adequately deal with companion animal death and will live a life tainted by sadness, loneliness, depression, anger, and unresolved grief. Even when your patients die, you can make a difference in your clients' lives by simply doing your best to help.

How to Provide Client Support

When it comes to dealing with companion animal death, you must understand the distinction between client support and grief counseling or grief therapy.

Client support, in this case, is defined as providing assistance to others before, during, and shortly following a death. Providing support is not long-term guidance, it is short-term assistance. Mainly, it consists of providing information and comfort.

Grief counseling, on the other hand, is the use of basic techniques to guide people through a normal, uncomplicated grief process to its successful completion. Grief therapy is the use of more complex, sophisticated intervention techniques to help people successfully negotiate a grief process that has become complicated or abnormal. Both grief counseling and grief therapy are roles for other health-care professionals.

Client Support Roles

When you support a client during pet loss and grief, you are not a psychiatrist, psychologist, social worker, family therapist, a member of

Figure 1
Normal Symptoms of Grief

Grief is more than feeling sad or depressed. Grief's influence is holistic and pervasive. For most people, grief manifests in physical, intellectual, emotional, social, and spiritual ways. Here is a short list:

- aching
- anger
- anxiety
- bargaining with or anger at God
- comparing the loss to others' losses
- confusion
- crying
- depression
- difficulties in communication
- difficulties with relationships
- difficulties with socializing
- disbelief
- disinterest in life
- distortions in time
- easily distracted
- eating changes
- exhaustion
- fatigue
- feeling overwhelmed
- feeling powerless
- feeling punished
- guilt
- hallucinations or visions
- illnesses
- irritability
- loneliness
- low motivation
- morbid thoughts
- nausea
- need to stay busy
- need to talk about loss
- numbness
- rationalization
- relief
- remorse
- restlessness
- sadness
- shaken spirituality or renewed spirituality
- shock
- sleep changes
- sobbing
- stiffness
- stomachaches
- tightness in chest
- trivializing the loss
- unpredictable mood swings
- vulnerability
- yearning

the clergy, or a suicide prevention counselor. These are professional roles that require years of study and experience. The client support strategies that comprise the bulk of this book are built upon four client support roles. They call for you to be an educator, supporter, facilitator, and a resource and referral guide. When a balance between these four roles is achieved, client support is usually effective.

1. Educator

Educate yourself about loss and grief. Observe, ask questions, and offer grief-related information when you feel pet owners need and can accept it. Remember, never force information on pet owners, but provide information to clients when the clients themselves are ready and willing to receive it. One way to do this is to make books, pamphlets, and videotapes available to clients so they can absorb information in a variety of ways and at their own pace.

2. Supporter

Support means listening to pet owners' non-medical concerns without taking action to solve their problems. Supporting clients means acknowledging their losses, giving them permission to express their thoughts and emotions, and listening to their pain as well as to their happy memories. Listening is an overlooked skill in veterinary medicine. Veterinarians often feel that they aren't being helpful unless they know how to solve their clients' problems. Yet, grieving pet owners often are more comforted by a listening ear than by well-meaning advice. Much of support is non-verbal. It is appropriate to show support by using touch, gestures, facial expressions, and direct eye contact in attentive, sensitive ways.

3. Facilitator

Facilitators ask questions, make suggestions, review medical information, and attempt to gain consensus on decisions. Remain neutral, non-judgmental, and respectful of pet owners' wishes. Never take charge, but provide enough structure to prevent emotions from interfering with the decisions that need to be made.

4. Resource and referral guide

Inform clients about the resources that are available to them and make recommendations about those which are most appropriate. Provide clients with information about how to contact resources, but let them do their own leg work. The more clients do for themselves, the more control they feel over their situations.

Client Support Principles

Effective support begins with respect for others and an awareness of the limits and boundaries of personal responsibility. Most client support strategies begin with empathy and understanding.

Empathy is having an intellectual and emotional comprehension of another person's condition without actually experiencing the other person's feelings. The concept of putting yourself in someone else's shoes is an example of empathy. You are being empathetic when you say, "I can imagine how sad you must feel, knowing that Samson might die."

Empathy is not sympathy. Sympathy is feeling sorry for someone. You are being sympathetic when you say, "Poor Susan! I feel so bad that you lost Samson today." Expressing sympathy for, or pitying, someone is not helpful when dealing with grief. Feeling pitied by others often offends people and is counter-productive to the understanding needed for effective support.

Client support strategies are strengthened when you understand that everyone possesses the knowledge and skills needed to negotiate their own grief. It is not helpful to rush in with personal ideas and agendas and take control of someone else's situation. (See Figure 2, page 18.) Rather, you can help facilitate the grieving process by offering clients guidance, structure, and honest information.

You can begin to develop a comfort level with grief by adhering to the basic client support principles by which paraprofessionals abide.

- Offer client support by mutual agreement. If your assistance is not wanted, back off.

- You cannot control how clients respond to loss; you can only control how you respond to clients.

- Never try to take someone's feelings away in order to make them feel better. People have a right to their feelings, whether or not you think they are justified.

- Behave according to a code of ethics. Convey information in honest, truthful ways; refuse to censor or withhold information to protect clients' feelings; and respect clients' rights to confidentiality.

- Know your limits, and never attempt to exceed the confines of your client support role. Seek resources for help when you need them, such as those listed at the end of this book.

Client Support Techniques

Provide information in a warm, clear, and honest way. Some of the techniques used to convey warmth and trustworthiness use the spoken word. Others use non-verbal techniques like direct eye contact, touch, facial expressions, and body language. To provide client support, you must be an effective communicator. This can be achieved by using ten basic verbal and non-verbal communication techniques. You will find these techniques referred to over and over again in the Client Support Strategies section.

Verbal Techniques

- **Acknowledging.** Acknowledging is recognizing the existence or truth of something. Acknowledging encourages people to deal openly and honestly with the emotions inside them and with the reality of the situation at hand. You might say, "I know you loved Ruby very much and that her death is very painful for you."

- **Normalizing.** Normalizing is lending credibility to others' thoughts, feelings, behaviors, and experiences. The symptoms of grief can seem quite disturbing when they are not clearly understood. Inform clients that it is normal for a wide range of emotions to accompany loss. You might say, "I would expect you to cry about Ruby. You two were together for 10 years and were best friends. It's normal to miss her."

- **Giving permission.** Giving permission means encouraging clients to think, feel, and behave however they need to (within safe limits) without fear of judgment. This technique also allows clients to ask for what they want or to make requests that are important to them. For instance, before euthanasia, clients may ask for a soft surface to lay their animals on, to be able to feed their pet one last time, or to be present when their pets die. You might say, "I know you and Ruby have shared a lot throughout your lives together. If there is anything you would like to do for her before she dies, please don't hesitate to tell me."

- **Asking appropriate questions.** Asking appropriate questions helps you gather valuable information about the circumstances surrounding your clients' loss. Failure to ask clients questions can lead to problems; there are many consequences to making assumptions about your clients' needs. The most helpful questions are open-ended, not closed-ended. A closed-ended question can be responded to with yes, no, fine, or some other one- or two-word answer. Open-ended questions elicit more detailed information and create opportunities for clients to tell you more about what they are experiencing. Open-ended questions begin with how or what rather than with why. How and what questions elicit thoughtful explanations. You might say, "How will you know when Ruby is no longer enjoying life?" Why questions often elicit "I don't know" answers. Why questions also have a tendency to put clients on the defensive, making them feel they need to explain themselves to you. One word of caution: A well-placed, open-ended question can launch a lengthy client monologue, so don't use them when you have a limited amount of time to spend with clients.

- **Paraphrasing.** Paraphrasing is the restatement or summary of a client's communication in order to test your understanding of their comments. When you paraphrase a client's comments, it reassures the client that the intended message got through. It also provides the client with the opportunity to clarify what was meant if your understanding is inaccurate. When paraphrasing words and emotions, it is important to paraphrase voice tone and pacing as well. For example, if a client is ranting loudly, you should respond in a voice that matches his in volume and energy. If you paraphrase anger using a quiet voice void of emotion, your client may feel you are being patronizing. This is likely to elicit more anger or even sarcasm from your client. As rapport develops and you gain some control over the situation, you can lower your voice and slow down your pace. This will, in turn, slow down your client's side of the conversation and create an atmosphere more conducive to helping. There are many ways to paraphrase. Easy ways to begin paraphrase statements are, "It seems as though …," "It sounds like …," and "If I hear you correctly, you feel …" A final way to use paraphrase is to summarize the main points of a lengthy conversation to ensure that you've understood your client's concerns. If your client says, "I don't know what I will do if Ruby dies while I'm not home. I'll never forgive myself," you might say, "You're worried that she'll die without you, and you'll feel guilty."

- **Self-disclosing.** Self-disclosing is briefly sharing a personal experience when it may be appropriate and of use to clients. Self-disclosing about your own experiences with companion animal death can help your clients feel less isolated. It can also normalize their grief. When using self-disclosure, it is very important not to shift the focus away from your client and onto yourself. You might say, "I lost both of my own cats to the same kind of cancer last year. Ruby's euthanasia was really hard for me, too."

> *Voice tone and pacing have the most influence on the meaning of spoken words.[17] For instance, if you use appropriate words to describe a situation but speak very fast, you may be seen as rushed, nervous, or insensitive. If you speak the same words too slowly, you may be viewed as dull or condescending. It is important for you to monitor your voice tone when you are working with clients who are grieving. Words that are spoken softly and at a slightly slower pace than normal are more comforting.*

Non-verbal Techniques

- **Structuring the environment.** Structuring the environment means paying attention to the various elements of your office, examination rooms, and consultation areas that can easily be moved and changed. It means paying attention to how chairs are arranged and how the furnishings in the room convey comfort, warmth, and understanding. The goal of structuring the environment is to invite your clients' emotions to arise, instead of shutting them down. You might place chairs so conversations can take place face-to-face without barriers like desks or examination tables between you and your clients. You might also adapt examination rooms so euthanasias can be performed on the examination table, the floor, or even on a gurney rolled near the window so the pet and pet owner can be near the outdoors.

When anxiety is high, people tend to get frozen into position. They forget they can stand up if they're sitting, walk around the room if they're standing, or even leave the room altogether if they need a few minutes to be alone. This rigidity can be overcome by adapting the physical elements of your environment to better meet the situation at hand.

- **Attending.** Attending uses body language to convey that careful attention is being paid to the person who is talking. When your body posture is open, your eye contact is direct, and you are leaning slightly forward toward the speaker, you are demonstrating your availability and willingness to be of service. Attending behaviors include non-judgmental facial expressions, encouraging gestures, affirmative head nods, and direct observation of what is occurring. You might sit down if your client sits down, or squat to be at children's eye level when greeting or talking to them.

- **Active listening.** Active listening means listening for feelings, rather than for the factual content of conversations. There is a difference between merely hearing someone and actively listening to what they say. Active listening incorporates paraphrasing, asking questions, and attending behaviors such as making eye contact and

Experts believe that only seven percent of communication happens verbally.[18] So, along with what is said, communication is where it is said, how it is said, why it is said, when it is said, who it is said to, and, let's not forget, what is not said. Non-verbal communication is conveyed through facial expressions, body postures, gestures, and hand movements, as well as through writing, reading, and listening.

Non-verbal communication adds meaning to the verbal. For example, if a person who is crying tells you they feel sad, you not only believe them, but probably feel a great deal of empathy for them. When these non-verbal communication techniques are used along with the previously discussed verbal ones, there is a much better chance that your message of compassion and care will be effectively conveyed.

using open body posture to encourage clients to say more. Two minor, but important, non-verbal communication techniques inherent in the process of active listening are necessary silences and minimal encouragers. Necessary silences take place when you remain silent while others vent their feelings or gather their thoughts rather than babble to fill the silent, empty spaces. Minimal encouragers are simple responses that encourage people to continue talking. Minimal encouragers let people know you are actively participating in the communication between you. They include head nods, eye blinks, and phrases like "Uh, huh," "I see," and "For instance?"

- **Responding with touch.** Responding with touch provides comfort, demonstrates care and concern, and often takes the place of reassuring words. Touch often has a calming effect and can help people slow their thoughts and steady themselves emotionally. There is some scientific evidence that touch affects the body physiologically, slowing heart rate and lowering blood pressure. Touch can be used to soothe a grieving client or to bring someone who is rambling back to the point. When using touch with clients, neutral or safe areas to touch are the shoulders and arms. Areas of the body that are not viewed as neutral or safe include the neck, hands, torso, lower back, and legs. In general, people dislike being patted on their backs or heads. This behavior implies a sense of superiority on your part and can be viewed as condescending. If touching or hugging clients makes you uncomfortable, a substitute technique is to touch your clients' companion animals with care. Pet owners often judge your sensitivity based on how you handle their pets.

Limits of Client Support

When you recognize the significance of the human-animal bond and become skilled at providing client support, you often develop an extremely loving and loyal clientele. Many of your clients will think of you as a friend. Once they have experienced the quality of your care, they may naturally turn to you for assistance with the other problems in their lives. For example, they may come to you with questions about an illness they are coping with, their child's struggle to recover from a severe injury, or the death of one of their close relatives or friends. These conversations will be emotional and it will be tempting for you to try to help in some way.

However, you must focus your efforts toward the issues that arise specific to the death of a companion animal. As much as you'd like to help Mary Jones learn to face the impending death of her elderly father, you are not trained to do so. Your job is to deal with the thoughts, feelings, behaviors, and issues associated with losing a beloved pet.

Figure 2
It is NOT Helpful to

- Use clichés such as "Time will heal." Clichés are simplistic solutions to complex problems. Using them tends to make people suppress, rather than express, their grief.

- Compare one griever's loss to another's. Comparisons are attempts to minimize the impact of loss and imply that the loss wasn't as bad as it could have been. Comparing tends to make people suppress, rather than express, their grief.

- Encourage grievers to stay busy to keep their minds off their grief. Grievers need slow, empty, alone time to fully experience their grief and move through it.

- Encourage grievers to make major changes in their lives. After a significant loss, many grievers consider moving, divorcing, or quitting their jobs. In general, though, grief clouds peoples' judgment. Decisions made too soon after loss may be regretted later.

- Attempt to cheer up grievers. Encouraging grievers to take vacations, go shopping, or to medicate their pain with alcohol or tranquilizing drugs encourages grievers to avoid reality. Avoiding the immediate symptoms of grief can ultimately lead to complicated, unresolved, and even pathological grief outcomes.

- Scold or give advice, lectures, or pep talks to grievers who are feeling down. Grief is a process that can take weeks, months, and even years to complete. Grievers need patience and understanding from their friends and family members.

- Suggest grievers replace the one they've lost. People who have experienced a major loss are often urged to get on with life and remarry, have another child, or adopt a new pet as soon as possible. Most grievers view this advice as insensitive and are deeply offended by the implication that anyone else could take the place of the unique loved one who died.

Client Support Strategies

How to Help in 15 Common Situations

Situation 1
Delivering the Bad News

> **You:** *"Mrs. Knight, I have some bad news that may be upsetting for you to hear."*
>
> **Client:** *"Oh, my goodness! Misty is dead, isn't she?"*
>
> **You:** *"Yes, Misty is dead. We did everything we could, but Misty died during surgery. I want you to know that she was anesthetized and felt no pain. We were with her when she died."*
>
> **Client:** *"Oh, Misty, Misty …I'm sorry! I shouldn't have brought you here. I should have taken you somewhere where they knew what they were doing!"*

What's Going on Here?

How clients will react when they receive bad news is largely unpredictable. Therefore, when you deliver bad news to clients, you should be prepared to deal with a wide range of grief responses like shock, disbelief, anger, sadness, and even hysteria. Anxiety and shock may cause one client to appear calm, stoic, or too much in control. He may say nothing, but engage in intensive hand-wringing and aimless pacing. Anxiety may cause another client to smile or laugh inappropriately, even when she has just learned her pet has died.

Still other clients may react with rage, guilt, or confusion. They may sob, scream, and even hit or kick objects that are in the room. A few clients, like the one introduced in the opening scenario, may accuse you of incompetence or even of making up a disease so you can charge them for expensive treatments. One or two may hang up on you if you're delivering bad news via the telephone, or some may simply turn and walk out your door, leaving the pet behind.

How Can I Help?

Many situations require that you give clients bad news. The most common situations include unexpected deaths, serious or terminal diagnoses, and euthanasia recommendations. Unfortunately, there are no magic strategies that allow you to break bad news painlessly. Thus, the delivery of bad news can be a stressful time for pet owners and veterinary professionals alike.

The delivery of bad news works best when you use a soft voice and speak more slowly than usual. It is also enhanced when discussions take place in a relaxed yet structured environment where you and your client can sit down, touch, and make direct eye contact. Crisis intervention experts recommend that a context of sensitivity and compassion be created when delivering bad news. They suggest that clients be emotionally prepared for what is to come. Those providing support should predict how clients may feel or respond when the news is given and then proceed to offer clients information in brief, step-by-step conversations. It takes time for most clients to fully realize the magnitude of what they have been told. Most will remember little about the first conversation they have with you and will have many questions to ask during the next.

If you were the veterinary professional in the opening conversation, it would be important for you to proceed by asking Mrs. Knight what she needs next. Some logical choices to offer her might be to provide her with more detailed medical information now or in an hour or so by calling or meeting with her again. You would also want to offer her the option of viewing Misty's body.

How Will I Know if I've Been Successful?

The best course of action when delivering bad news is to provide your clients with the basic facts and then listen and attend to their emotional responses without becoming defensive, guilty, or angry yourself. This is a tall order but possible to accomplish if you understand grief. In most cases, when clients respond inappropriately to loss, they are not aware of how their words and behaviors may affect you. They are simply reacting, manifesting their grief. Later, when they realize what they have said or done, the majority of clients feel embarrassed and apologetic. When you understand grief, you can normalize their behaviors and forgive grieving clients for taking their feelings about the situation out on you.

Figure 3
Telephone Etiquette for Delivering Bad News

There are several common courtesies you should abide by when using the telephone to deliver bad news. They are:

- Prepare yourself for potentially emotional calls by finding a quiet, controlled environment where you won't be distracted or interrupted.

- If you don't reach your client, do not leave details about emotional topics like a pet's death, relapse, or body care arrangements on voice mail or answering machines. Just leave a message, asking your client to return your call.

- Maintain your client's confidentiality. If another family member or a co-worker answers or even returns your call, don't give them the details about your patient's condition. Simply leave the same message, asking your client to return your call, or call back yourself at another time.

- If a client has not returned your call within a reasonable amount of time, call again. Messages get lost and clients, especially emotional ones, sometimes forget to return calls. It's your responsibility to make contact with your client, and you must keep trying until that task is accomplished.

- When you call a client at work, he or she may be unable to talk freely with you about emotional issues at that time as they may not have any privacy. Before you begin, tell them you need to discuss a difficult issue with them and ask them if this is a convenient time to talk or if they would prefer to arrange a telephone appointment when they can speak more freely from a private area.

- Give clients choices regarding how much detail and the kind of information you share with them. For example, you might say, "I would be happy to explain the details of Misty's surgery to you. Would you like that information now?" Each client's need for details varies, so it's best to ask rather than overwhelm your client with information.

Quick Tips

What to Say, What to Do

- Expect to deal with a wide range of grief responses, from angry accusations to complete silence.

- Structure the environment. Before delivering bad news, stock a private area with tissues and arrange furniture so you can sit down and talk face-to-face. Never deliver bad news in a public area.

- Practice saying words like died and dead so you can deliver bad news without stumbling awkwardly over the words. It is not helpful to use euphemisms when discussing bad news.

- Deliver bad news in three stages. 1) Prepare clients emotionally for what is to come, 2) predict how clients may feel or respond when the news is given, and 3) proceed to offer clients information in brief, step-by-step increments. For example:

  1) "Mrs. Knight, I have some bad news …"

  2) … that may be upsetting for you to hear."

  3) "Yes, Misty is dead. We did everything we could, but Misty died during surgery. I want you to know that she was anesthetized and felt no pain. We were with her when she died."

- Touch, attend, and paraphrase to de-escalate tension and calm the client.

- Acknowledge your client's emotions and don't take their comments personally. For example, to respond to Mrs. Knight's accusation, you might say, "It sounds like you're angry that Misty died, Mrs. Knight. I'd be angry if my dog had just died, too. We provided Misty with the highest quality of care, but her injuries were so severe and extensive that they caused her death. I'm sad that she died, too."

My Notes

Situation 2
Crises and Emergencies

> *Rhonda rushes her dog Romeo to your veterinary clinic on a Friday afternoon at 4:45 p.m. Romeo has just been hit by a car, his injuries are severe, and his life is in danger. Romeo needs immediate treatment, but Rhonda is clutching him to her chest and will not give you the dog.*
>
> *"My husband and I are divorcing, and Romeo is the first thing my son looks for when he comes home from school. You have to fix Romeo!" she shouts. "If he's not there, I don't know what my son will do!"*
>
> *By this time, Rhonda is crying and her voice has taken on an edge of desperation. Still cradling Romeo, she begins to pace across the waiting room, but, with a sudden burst of anger, she returns to you and shoves Romeo into your arms. She screams, "Go fix him! Don't just stand there! Go fix him!" Then she collapses onto her knees and sobs.*

What's Going On Here?

Rhonda is in crisis. Crises cause people to function in ways that are not normal for them. When people are in crisis, many feel out of control, panicked, angry, and confused. They experience time as either moving very quickly or very slowly. Crisis makes it hard for people to listen and to later recall information.

When people are in crisis, they display symptoms of shock and anxiety. Many are unable to think clearly or to follow directions. In the acute stage of crisis, some people behave in erratic or irrational ways. When people are in crisis, the skills and knowledge they normally use to cope with life are either forgotten or no longer work. Crises escalate when people feel helpless and can't find effective ways to respond to the events that are unfolding.

How Can I Help?

The purpose of providing client support during crisis is to direct people toward an acceptable resolution for their problem. Generally, the two main goals during crisis are 1) to stabilize the situation and assist your client in returning to normal and 2) to assist your client as she finds her own solutions to her problems.

When providing support during crisis, it is important to assist your client with the situation at hand while at the same time assessing what her needs might be at a later time. For example, you may want to link your client to any community resources such as veterinary medical specialists or pet loss support groups that can continue to assist her in the days and weeks ahead.

During a crisis, it is important to pay attention to what clients say they want and need, in addition to what you might think they want and need. When clients feel that their needs are validated, they relax more, develop more trust in you, and are better able to listen to and make decisions about the medical options you offer them.

Clinical experience shows that clients who are deprived of contact with their ill or injured companion animals usually become more anxious and demanding. Everyone's needs are better served when clients are invited and even encouraged to visit their pets while they are hospitalized. This is especially important if the prognosis is poor, and the patient isn't expected to live.

If you are concerned about your client's response to seeing her pet hooked up to emergency equipment and monitors, take time to prepare her for what she will see. For most pet owners, visiting their pets or having the chance to say good-bye to them one last time far outweighs any anxiety they may have about seeing their pets in critical condition.

Keep in Mind

- Sometimes people other than the owner bring animals to your clinic. These animals have usually been injured without their owners' knowledge. If these John Doe animals have no identifying information, consider photographing them so that, if they die, they might later be identified.

- When a crisis reaches a conclusion, make sure your client is calm and stable enough to drive home. It's difficult to function during a crisis, and even second-nature activities like driving can feel overwhelming for some people. Sometimes it's best to encourage your client to call a friend or family member to drive them home.

How Will I Know if I've Been Successful?

As a veterinary professional, you will feel most successful when you are able to save the life of the animal brought to you during a medical emergency. Yet, even if your patient dies, when your client thanks you for waiting with her, tells you that she appreciated your frequent medical updates, or simply lets you know that she truly felt cared about, you will know that your helping efforts made a difference in her emotional life. And the odds are in your favor that she will return to your practice in the future.

My Notes

Quick Tips

What to Say, What to Do

- Respond immediately to any crisis. Pay attention to your client's emotional needs as well as to the animal's medical needs.

- Use touch and a soothing voice to calm your client.

- Acknowledge your client's emotions. Give permission to express them, by saying, for example, "I see how much you love Romeo. I would expect you to cry in this situation."

- Structure the environment by gently, yet firmly, guiding your client to an office, an examination room, or even a treatment room, depending on the medical status of the animal. If your client insists upon carrying the pet, allow this, place a firm arm around her shoulders, and quickly walk with her to wherever you need to go.

- Once treatment has begun, designate one staff person (one who is not involved in providing direct treatment for the animal) to facilitate your client's emotional support. This person should notify other clients about the emergency and reschedule their appointments, if necessary; wait with your client while the pet's medical condition is being evaluated; keep your client well-informed about the pet's medical status while treatment is taking place; and offer your client tissues, a glass of water, and a telephone so she can notify other family members regarding the emergency.

Situation 3
Decision-making

> **Client:** *"I don't know what I should do. I promised Candy I would always make the decision that was best for her, but I don't know what that is. If Candy were your dog, what would you do?"*

What's Going on Here?

Decision-making is one of the most difficult tasks that pet owners face. Whether the decision is fairly inconsequential (e.g., vaccinations, dental exams, diagnostic tests) or extremely serious (e.g., surgery, amputation, expensive treatments, euthanasia), many pet owners get stuck in the decision-making process and ask for additional guidance from you. Yet, clients who ask the question featured in the opening scenario are not only looking for your medical opinion, they are also looking for reassurance. They want to know that you will support them regardless of the decision they make.

The problem with this situation is that most clients want to please the professionals with whom they work and be viewed as cooperative, responsible clients. Thus, based on your recommendation, your client may move ahead with the decision to euthanize her pet even though she is not yet ready to let go. Later, that same client may feel you pressured her into euthanizing her animal. When clients believe their veterinarians rushed them through the process of saying good-bye and helping their pet die, it can cause irreparable damage to the veterinarian-client relationship.

Rather than stating your personal opinion, you might say, "If Candy were my dog, I would be confused and upset, just like you are. Euthanasia is one of the most difficult decisions you will ever make in your life, and the fact is that you and I will probably be ready to face it at slightly different times. Even if I believe the time is right to help Candy die, you must also believe it, or it will be difficult for you to feel at peace with your decision." Or you might say, "The truth is, Candy isn't my dog, and what I might do and what you might do could be very different. You are the expert on Candy. No matter what you decide, I'll support you and your decision."

How Can I Help?

Decision-making may be the area of helping where educating, facilitating, and offering sources of support and referral are most valuable. The minutes, hours, days, or weeks leading up to making a significant decision are among the most anxious times pet owners experience. Anxiety can make decisions even harder to make.

There are several decision-making techniques you can use to help your clients arrive at the decisions that are right for them and their companion animals. They include:

1. Thinking through the consequences. Help your clients think through as many different scenarios as apply, so they can make informed choices based on the outcome they would prefer. For example, you might say, "I know it's difficult to actually make an appointment to euthanize Candy. However, I want you to think about the consequences if we don't schedule a time. The first outcome may be that she may die while you're at work or away from the house. In this scenario, she may be in pain and die alone. In addition, you would be the one to find her body and may feel, at that time, that she didn't have the kind of death you wanted for her. The second scenario to consider is that, if you don't schedule an appointment now and wait until her condition becomes an emergency, I may not be the veterinarian on duty and may not be the one to perform the euthanasia."

2. Asking tough questions. If your client seems stuck in the decision-making process, use attending behaviors and active listening skills to draw out her concerns. If a decision still can't be reached, you may need to ask a few tough questions designed to help your client recognize the reality of her pet's situation. These are probing questions and must be asked without any judgment in your voice. Preface your questions with a comment like, "I am going to ask you something that is hard for me to say and may be difficult for you to hear." Then ask, "Are you telling yourself that this decision will be easier to make tomorrow or several days or weeks from now?" or "If you choose not to euthanize Candy, are you putting her needs ahead of your own, or are you putting your needs ahead of hers?" Be careful when you ask this last question! It must be asked very gently and with no judgment in your voice or in your facial expressions.

3. The illusion of choice and providing a back door. In most cases, helping your client make a small choice will direct her toward the outcome you desire, yet still give her some feeling of control. You could say, "I know you've decided to euthanize Candy, Dawn, but you're still struggling with when to schedule the procedure. For Candy's sake and with your agreement, I would like to make the appointment for tomorrow. Would two or four o'clock work best for you?" If your client becomes more anxious once she has made a definite commitment to a course of action, you can conclude this technique by providing your client with a back door. A back door is a way to cancel her agreement. You could say, "If you find you simply can't go through with the procedure, Dawn, you can always change your mind and reschedule your appointment for another time."

4. Identifying bottom lines. A bottom line is a guideline by which your client can measure the factors that must be considered to make a decision. Bottom lines are different for everyone. When it comes to a decision like whether or not to euthanize a pet, your client's bottom line might be her dog's inability to enjoy normal activities, her pet's level of pain and discomfort, the length of time her dog is expected to live, or even the cost of continuing to treat the animal. You might ask her, "Dawn, many pet owners find it helpful to imagine the circumstances that would need to arise for them to make this decision. I call this thinking about your bottom line. For some clients, the bottom line is their pet's inability to walk or to get up under her own power. For others, it's a change in the way their pet responds to them. Do you have an idea of what the bottom line might be for you and Candy?"

5. Enlisting a pet's help. When your client and her companion animal have a deep, special relationship, there is also a unique form of communication between them. When a decision regarding the pet's welfare needs to be made, you can encourage your client to enlist her pet's help, so she doesn't feel she is making the decision alone. You could tell her, "Dawn, you and Candy have always been able to communicate. That hasn't changed. Even now, if you get down on the floor, lay beside Candy, and look into her eyes, she may tell you what she wants you to do. Together, you can make this decision about how and when we should help her die."

How Will I Know if I've Been Successful?

Your client support efforts will be successful when your clients make the decisions that are right for them and their companion animals, even though they may not always be the decisions you want your clients to make!

Quick Tips

What to Say, What to Do

- Acknowledge your client's relationship with her pet and the immediate circumstances that make the decision difficult. You might say, "I know Candy is like a child to you, and you feel protective about her."

- Validate the difficulty of the decision-making process and your commitment to support your client's decision. You might say, "I realize this is one of the hardest decisions you've ever had to make regarding Candy's welfare."

- If you need a quick decision because of an animal's deteriorating medical condition, structure the environment by providing your client with a private place to think, some paper and a pencil so she can list the pros and cons of each option, and a telephone so she can consult with a friend or a family member. Be sure to tell her when you will need her decision. You might say, "Dawn, I wish I could give you more time, but based on Candy's condition and my schedule, I'll need your decision in 20 minutes."

- If there are no medical reasons requiring a quick decision, give your client permission to take hours or even days to make a decision.

- Once a decision has been made, paraphrase your client's words and feelings to ensure you are both committed to the same course of action. You might say, "It sounds like you want me to proceed with the euthanasia. I hear your anxiety, and I also hear that you feel it is the most humane act we can make on Candy's behalf. Am I hearing you correctly?"

My Notes

Situation 4
Client-present Euthanasia

Dear Dr. Vogel,

We just want you to know that we appreciate everything you've done for us over the years that you've been Buddy's veterinarian. Buddy was very special to us, and we thank you for your patience and compassion during his last hours. That his death was peaceful and that we were able to say good-bye to him in such a personal way meant a great deal to us. Thank you for the skilled, sensitive way you helped Buddy die.

We will be moving to the other side of town soon, but we plan to continue to bring our remaining pets, Misty and Jake, to your clinic. You are a valued part of our family medical support system, and we won't let a few miles separate us from the important care you provide. Thanks again.

The Mathews Family

What's Going on Here?

Today, more and more pet owners want to be with their companion animals when they die, and most veterinarians graciously accommodate their clients' wishes. Because the trend toward client-present euthanasia is so strong, it is essential that you develop euthanasia techniques and protocols that take into account not only the physical needs of your animal patients, but the psychological, emotional, and even spiritual needs of your human clients as well. While euthanasia procedures have traditionally been performed in an impersonal, clinical way as a means to protect both veterinarians and clients from painful emotions, a euthanasia performed with technical skill and sensitivity, respect for your clients' emotional needs, and compassionate support, represents one of the best opportunities you have to create a lasting bond with your clients.

How Can I Help?

Today, euthanasia is viewed as a professional privilege and as a gift that can be bestowed upon dying patients. Many companion animals are euthanized with their human family members in attendance, in the context of a respectful and reverent ceremony. This compassionate act requires veterinarians to develop a deep understanding of the human-animal bond, of the needs of grieving pet owners, and of the components of a skilled and sensitive euthanasia technique.

In this modern model of euthanasia, veterinary professionals thoroughly discuss euthanasia with their clients and involve them in the process as much as possible. Pet owners are also encouraged to talk openly about their companion animals after death has occurred. The new paradigm is both practical and compassionate. It is based on interdisciplinary research and clinical experience that describes the components necessary to create both healthy grief resolution and effective practice management.

It's important for you to remember that not all of your clients will want or require a lot of time or attention during their pets' euthanasias. Based on clinical experience, each client will make different choices. Some will choose total involvement and will orchestrate a fairly complex euthanasia ceremony. Others will choose minimal involvement, opting for only a good-bye hug as they leave their animal with you. However, all clients will appreciate being given the option to be as actively involved as they choose to be in the euthanasia planning process and in the actual procedure.

The key words when conducting euthanasias within the new paradigm are choice and preparation. You can assist pet owners in making wise and timely decisions when faced with their pets' deaths by providing them with information and options. Your role during this time is to provide detailed information about the process of euthanasia and to demonstrate non-judgmental support during the decision-making process.

When clients elect to be present when their pets die, the words you choose and the actions you take are critical. There are three basic components of an effective client-present euthanasia technique: 1) respectful preparation, 2) sensitive facilitation, and 3) supportive closure.

1. Respectful preparation

- Introduce the option of euthanasia as soon as it is a viable medical option. Explain the emotional aspects, as well as the medical details and give owners choices regarding how they want to be involved in the death.

  For example, you might say, "Mrs. Mathews, I know Buddy is very important to you and to your family. Therefore, I am committed to making his death as meaningful and as positive for you as possible. To decide whether or not you want to be with Buddy when he dies, you need accurate information about how I conduct euthanasia ceremonies. Would you like me to explain the procedures I use now?"

  With the owner's permission, you can continue with a step-by-step description of the medical details, while painting a comforting picture of how the client can be involved with the pet. For example, you might say, "While I do what I need to accomplish, you can pet or hold Buddy's head and paws. You can also talk to him, sing softly, or recite a poem or a prayer. In addition, you can play music, light a candle, or anything else that helps you. In other

---

Quick Tips

What to Say, What to Do

- Acknowledge clients immediately when they arrive for their pet's euthanasia. Don't expect them to wait in a busy, relatively upbeat waiting room on such a sad occasion.

- Structure the environment so the euthanasia site is conducive to saying emotional good-byes. This might include providing a soft surface for the pet to lie on, lowering the lighting in the room, and doing whatever is necessary to ensure your client's privacy.

- Give your clients permission to feel whatever emotions they are feeling as the time for euthanasia approaches. This may include giving them permission to express difficult emotions like anxiety, fear, and anger. One way to do this is by joining with them in the emotion. You might say, "I know you're angry that our attempts to treat Buddy failed, Mrs. Mathews. I'm angry, too. I wish we could have bought more time for Buddy with the chemotherapy."

- Attend to your clients' emotions before proceeding with the medical details of euthanasia.

- Use self-disclosure to create rapport with your clients and to let them know what they might expect from you as the euthanasia progresses. For example, if you tend to cry when your patients die, you might say, "I want you to know I'm a person who cries easily, and I'm likely to shed a few tears today when I help Buddy die. I will still be able to do my job, though, and make sure that you have the opportunities you need to say good-bye to Buddy however you wish."

- Ask questions and use active listening before, during, and after the euthanasia procedure to ensure that, to the best of your ability, your client's needs are being met.

- Use touch to comfort, focus, and stabilize your clients emotionally. You can also use touch (a supportive hand on your client's arm, your arm around your client's shoulders, even hugs) to express your own condolences

words, I want you to do whatever you need to do to feel you have said good-bye to Buddy in the most meaningful way possible."

- Deal with logistical matters, like signing consent forms, paying for the procedure, and making arrangements for body care, prior to the day of euthanasia, if possible.

- When clients arrive for the euthanasia, don't leave them to sit in a busy waiting area. Instead, immediately take them to the agreed-upon euthanasia site.

2. Sensitive facilitation

- Before the euthanasia procedure takes place, give pet owners the opportunity to spend a short time alone with their companion animals, if they so desire. Pet owners often report that they feel rushed through the euthanasia process and feel this negated the other positive aspects of their expectations.

- If pet owners have elected to be present, the use of a catheter is highly recommended. Even if you hit a vein 99 percent of the time, there are times when the Fates go against you. If you have to poke several times for a vein, animals naturally begin to pull away from you. Pet owners can interpret this as their companion animal struggling to stay alive. They may even feel that you are needlessly hurting their pet.

Catheters are not always necessary and do not always improve the medical procedures involved with euthanasia. However, they are often an enhancement to the emotional side of euthanasia because they provide extra insurance that pet owners will leave your clinic with the perception that their animal died peacefully, without any struggle.

If you decide to use a catheter, it should be placed in the animal's rear leg so the owner can be near the pet's head. If you are concerned about the added cost of using catheters for euthanasias, nonsterile, previously used ones can be placed. You might explain this aspect of your technique by saying, "The first thing I will do to prepare for Buddy's euthanasia is to take him to the treatment area, shave a small area of fur on one of his rear legs, and place an intravenous catheter. The use of a catheter simply means that I can make the necessary injections more smoothly."

- Years of clinical experience conducting thousands of client-present euthanasias at Colorado State University's Veterinary Teaching Hospital have shown that, when clients are present, using a series of injections is preferable to the sole use of a euthanasia solution.

The series most often used by clinicians at Colorado State University Veterinary Teaching Hospital includes 1) a saline flush to test the catheter, 2) a barbiturate, usually thiopental, to relax the animal, and 3) the euthanasia solution, usually pentobarbital sodium. Using a drug combination like thiopental and pentobarbital sodium seems to minimize any possible side effects, making the animal's death as peaceful and painless as possible.

A technique that requires that you make three injections is another reason to use a catheter. You can explain why you are repeatedly injecting an animal by saying something like, "The euthanasia method I prefer to use involves three injections. The first is a saline solution flush. This tells me that the catheter is working. The second is a barbiturate, which places Buddy into a soothing state of relaxation. The third injection is the euthanasia solution. This injection will actually stop Buddy's heart, brain activity, and other bodily functions, and ultimately cause his death. His death will take place within a matter of seconds." While you are injecting the animal, be discreet with needles and syringes. (Keep them in the pocket of a laboratory coat or a smock and return them there after each injection is completed.) The sight of needles causes great anxiety in some clients.

- Even though this recommended euthanasia technique (the use of a catheter and drug combination) usually minimizes any possible side effects, they can still occur. Therefore, you should predict that they might be part of the client-present euthanasia experience. You can do this by saying something like, "You should also know that, although my technique is designed to eliminate them, there may be some side effects of the drugs. For instance, Buddy may urinate, defecate, twitch, or even sigh a bit after he dies. He will not be aware of any of this, though, and he will not feel any pain. In addition, Buddy's eyes will most likely remain open. Muscles close our eye, and once death has occurred, Buddy will not have use of these muscles."

- Before you begin the injections, tell the owner that you are ready to proceed.

- Once the procedure has begun, the drugs should be injected quickly, with little or no lapse of time between them. As they are injected, each should be named so owners are kept abreast of how the procedure is progressing. For example, you might say, "Mrs. Mathews, I am injecting the first solution, the saline flush, to make sure the catheter I have inserted is working properly." Once that has been done, the next might be announced by saying, "Now I am giving

Buddy a barbiturate that will make him sleepy and help him drift off and relax." When it is time for the last injection, you might say, "Now I am injecting the final drug."

Aside from these statements, it's best for you to remain silent. Most owners want to focus on saying good-bye to their animals and find comments, questions, and chatter distracting to their concentration.

3. Supportive closure

- This method of facilitating euthanasia usually goes so quickly and smoothly that most owners don't realize when their pets have actually died. It is very important, then, for you to use a stethoscope to listen for a final heartbeat. This visible act reassures pet owners that their companion animal has truly died. After listening for a heartbeat, when you can do so with certainty, the animal should also be pronounced dead. You should do this by gaining direct eye contact with your client and stating in a clear, soft voice, "Mrs. Mathews, Buddy is dead." At this time, owners may gasp, cry, or sigh with relief. They may make remarks about how quickly death came and about how peaceful the experience was.

- After death has occurred, you can reassure your client about the decision to euthanize the animal. You can also express your own feelings of affection for the pet. For example, you might say, "I'm going to miss Buddy, too. He always wagged his tail for me." These statements may then prompt a spontaneous review of the pet's life with pet owners sharing their special stories with you.

- After euthanasia, some pet owners want to leave the site quickly, while others need more time alone with their pets. Whenever possible, accommodate your client's needs. Don't assume pet owners will want to be alone with their pets' bodies. Always ask your clients what they prefer.

Keep in Mind

- Anxiety is usually high just prior to and during euthanasia. Sometimes owners have momentary episodes of panic. If this happens, it is best for you to halt the procedure and attend to your client's emotions before continuing. You can say something like, "This is always the most anxious and difficult moment, Mrs. Mathews, but we have all decided this is best for Buddy. Let's take a deep breath and say good-bye one more time." It goes without saying that, if clients become adamant about stopping the procedure, it should be stopped, if it is still medically possible to do so. In many years of

clinical experience, though, very few practitioners have ever encountered this situation.

- Many pet owners prefer euthanasias to be conducted at their homes. Offering home euthanasia requires you to expend more of your time and staff resources, so you should charge accordingly. Pet owners are understanding about the extra effort home euthanasia requires, and most are willing to pay more for the service.

  Two important things about conducting home euthanasias: Be prepared to deal with strong emotions, and remember to take multiple quantities of everything you might need for the procedure so you won't be caught without a necessary item.

- Sometimes circumstances call for modifications in the client-present euthanasia technique recommended in this strategy. For example, the veins of very old or ill cats often cannot be catheterized. If a deviation in technique occurs, it's important that you explain it to clients and prepare them for any consequences that may arise.

- Contrary to tradition, owners of large animals can also benefit from being present at their companion animal's euthanasia. However, since the deaths of horses, llamas, cattle, and other large animals often involve more disturbing side effects (like bodies collapsing suddenly to the ground, involuntary movements, and agonal breaths after death has occurred), owners should be well-prepared for what they might witness. However, once they have been educated about the difficult circumstances surrounding large animal euthanasia, they should be allowed to choose their own level of involvement.

How Will I Know if I've Been Successful?

The best indicator of an effective and sensitive euthanasia technique is a satisfied and relieved client. Many clients who have been present at their pet's euthanasia make comments like, "I feel sad that he's dead, but happy that we could give him such a gentle death," and "I never knew that witnessing death could be so helpful. I feel like I can let go of him now, knowing he died so peacefully."

Grateful clients often want to give something back to the veterinary professionals who helped them and their pets at such a crucial time. Thus, they send thank you notes, gifts of appreciation, and donations to the practice. They also tell their friends about you. A noticeable boost in your business, due to a reputation for being sensitive and compassionate, is the ultimate success.

Figure 4
Checklist for Client-present Euthanasia Procedures

Use these steps as a guide to assist clients with ceremonial owner-present euthanasia.

1. Respectful preparation. Before the procedure, have you:

_____ Informed clients about the methods used to conduct euthanasia?

_____ Prepared clients for what may happen during the procedure? (e.g., possible drug side effects, their own grief manifestations)

_____ Offered clients a choice about being present?

_____ Helped plan the logistical details of euthanasia? (e.g., where, when, body care, body container, bringing a friend for support)

_____ Offered reading materials, informational videotapes, facility tours, and referrals, where appropriate?

_____ Asked clients to sign consent forms and pay bills ahead of time?

_____ Notified other clients who are waiting for appointments that there may be unexpected delays?

2. Sensitive facilitation. During the procedure, have you:

_____ Asked another veterinary professional to assist you?

_____ Prepared the euthanasia site?

_____ Placed a catheter?

_____ Offered clients time alone with their pets?

_____ Pronounced the animal dead?

_____ Allowed clients to clip fur, remove collars, or carry through with any activity that may be symbolic and meaningful to them?

3. Supportive closure. After the procedure, have you:

_____ Positioned/prepared the body for viewing, storage, or transport?

_____ Informed clients about the grief they are likely to experience?

_____ Escorted clients out a side or rear door?

_____ Updated client files and records?

_____ Sent condolence cards or letters?

_____ Made follow-up telephone calls?

_____ Made referrals to support groups or counselors, if appropriate?

_____ Planned debriefing or stress management strategies?

If you tend to get anxious during client-present euthanasias, keep this checklist handy on a clipboard or inside a client file. Discreetly refer to it, if needed.

My Notes

Situation 5
Non-euthanasia Deaths: Saying Good-bye/Viewing Bodies

You: *"Helen, I know that the thought of seeing Pixie's body is difficult, but I want to assure you that there is a strong correlation between viewing a loved one's body and the progression of normal, healthy grief."*

Helen: *"I do want to see Pixie. It's just that the thought of it makes me nervous. I've never seen a dead body before."*

You: *"I'll be happy to go with you when you see her, Helen. Would you like me to do that, or would you prefer to go into the room alone?"*

Helen: *"Oh, I'd appreciate it if you'd stay with me."*

You: *"I'd be happy to stay with you. Now, before we go to Pixie, let me prepare you a bit for what you'll see and be able to do. When you see Pixie, her body will still be warm, her eyes will be open, and her tongue may protrude slightly from her mouth. Pixie is covered with a blanket from her head down, but you may remove it if you want to see her entire body. As you remember, there are stitches on Pixie's abdomen where we made the incision during surgery. It's all right for you to touch Pixie, to pet her, and even hold her if you want to. However, her body may be slightly soiled due to the release of her bowel and bladder. There is a brush and a scissors in the room if you want to groom her or clip some of her fur to take with you."*

What's Going on Here?

Sometimes clients or other family members who weren't present when a pet died may want to view the animal's body before it is buried or cremated. You should encourage this. Grief experts agree that seeing a dead body helps people accept the reality of death. It also allows pet owners to say a final good-bye to their pets.

If a pet's body is going to be viewed after death, clients need to be prepared for what they will see and feel. They also need guidance regarding what will be acceptable for them to do. The conversation in the opening scenario is an example of some of the words, phrases, and concepts you might use to prepare a client to view a pet's body.

How Can I Help?

Research shows it's beneficial for grievers to view a loved one's body. When you are providing grief support, it's often up to you to make this experience a positive one. When a client wishes to view his pet's body, clean the body of any blood or waste material and position it so the pet will be pleasing for the owners to see. The body should be curled slightly, with the head and limbs tucked into a sleep-like position. This is most easily accomplished by placing the body in a container of some sort. Place the body on a blanket, fleece, or a soft pad and cover it from the neck down, leaving the face and head exposed so the owner can see and talk to his pet.

Positioning a body is especially important if it is to be placed into a casket or other container for burial or transport at a later time or if you are keeping the animal's body in a cooler until other family members can view it or pick it up. If animals, particularly large dogs, are allowed to stiffen without being curled into a sleep-like position, placing them in a casket or even on the back seat of a car is nearly impossible. For this reason, it's a good idea to keep a box, a vinyl casket, or another container at your clinic for viewing and storage purposes.

If clients ask you to accompany them while they view their pet's body, lead the way into the examination room or visitation site and make the first move toward touching, petting, and talking to the animal. This is a prime time to act as a role model for your clients so they will have a better idea of what to do. After you've spent some time talking with and listening to your clients, ask if they would like some time alone. If the answer is yes, leave the room and tell them how soon you plan to return.

If the owner is not taking his or her pet's body after viewing it, you or another staff member should stay with the animal's body at the site. Often owners will take one last look back at their pet before actually leaving. When they see a familiar face next to their pet, they feel reassured that their companion animal's body will not be forgotten or treated with disrespect once they leave.

How Will I Know if I've Been Successful?

When clients have been well-prepared to view a body and have been given the time to say a private, personal good-bye, they will almost always thank you. Even though anticipating a viewing often creates anxiety, the actual viewing of a body usually provides relief. Creating the opportunity to view a loved one's body and offering clients the choice to do so is an extremely effective aspect of your helping role. You will know you've been successful when clients later tell you that viewing their pet's body allowed them to finish business or draw closure to their relationship, or simply say a heartfelt good-bye. All are necessary parts of a normal grief process.

Quick Tips

What to Say, What to Do

- Acknowledge and normalize anxiety. You might say, "I know that the thought of seeing Pixie's body is difficult."

- Educate clients about the link between viewing a body and the progression of grief. You might say, "We know there is a strong correlation between viewing a loved one's body and the progression of normal, healthy grief."

- Prepare for a visitation. Remove any tape or medical equipment from the animal's body, clean away any blood or waste material, place the body on a soft blanket or pad, and cover or wrap the body in a blanket or towel, leaving the head exposed.

- Give clients permission to touch, hold, and talk to their pet.

- Don't assume clients would like time alone with their pet unless they agree to it. Once they seem comfortable viewing and touching the body, ask again if they would like some time alone.

My Notes

Situation 6
Crying Clients

> **Client:** *"I'm so sorry I'm crying. I shouldn't be crying …"*
>
> **You:** *"It's okay to cry, Mary. I'd cry, too, if I had just learned that my dog had cancer."*

What's Going on Here?

Crying is one of the classic symptoms of grief. People cry when they are grieving because it is a natural reaction to pain. Crying is an effective way to release emotion and an essential part of the grieving process. Still, like the client in the opening dialogue, many people feel embarrassed or ashamed of their emotional outbursts.

Dr. William Frey, a biochemist considered to be the leading authority on human tears, says, "People have the right to be human, to feel, to cry. They need to know there is no need to deprive themselves of the natural, healthy, release of emotional tears."

One of the biggest obstacles to helping others when they cry is the fear that you may cry, too. Unfortunately, many conversations take place in which veterinary professionals discourage clients from being present at their pets' euthanasias because they are afraid they themselves might cry and lose control in a professional situation.

Their fear is that, if they are upset, they won't know what to say or what to do to help their grieving clients. Clients rarely report that they disliked it when a staff member cried with them. In fact, it touches clients deeply when you cry with them.

How Can I Help?

People generally feel better after crying. In one study, researchers found that widows who had friends who encouraged them to cry were healthier than widows who experienced less encouragement from others to cry and to discuss their feelings of grief. It follows, then, that the best way you can support your crying clients is to encourage them to get it out. Allow them to sniffle, sob, or wail. If clients exhibit extreme displays of emotion, like sobbing or panic attacks, help them work through their waves of emotion. Never leave the room because you assume your clients want to be alone. The act of leaving the room may signal your own embarrassment or disapproval of their grief. All forms of crying are healthy and acceptable. Your job when providing client support is to become comfortable with tears.

There are different kinds of tears. Dr. Frey reports that tears stirred by onions or dirt and tears stirred by sadness or joy do not have the same chemical content. Emotional tears contain more protein than irritant tears. They also contain elevated amounts of hormones and neurotransmitters. Why they differ is unclear, but Dr. Frey theorizes that emotional tears remove substances released into our bodies during times of stress. Just as exhaling and perspiring help maintain homeostasis in our bodies by removing waste and harmful substances, so do emotional tears.

How Will I Know if I've Been Successful?

Many veterinary medical professionals do cry when their patients die. It is important to remember that emotional displays are normal responses to loss and grief. People who cry usually need permission to express their feelings and need to be reassured that they are normal. This is true for you, as well. One of the most frequent comments clients make is, "It meant so much to me that the doctor (or nurse or receptionist) cried, too. I could tell how much my pet meant to him/her."

My Notes

Quick Tips

What to Say, What to Do

- Acknowledge your client's tears. You might say, "I can see how sad you are about Freddie's diagnosis."

- Normalize your client's tears. You might say, "I would expect you to cry in a situation like this."

- Give permission to cry. Offer your client a tissue and a place to sit down, saying "Take your time, and let it out, Mary. I'm right here if you need me."

- Touch your client, if providing non-verbal comfort is appropriate.

- Self-disclose by crying yourself if you're moved to do so. Crying demonstrates compassion and shows empathy for pets and their owners. If you cry easily, you might say, "I often cry during times like this. I can still do my job, though, and be here for you."

Situation 7
Helping Children

> **Parent:** *"Jimmy, Dr. Milman couldn't save Midas. He was too badly hurt when the car hit him, and he's gone now. We can't see him anymore."*
>
> **Jimmy:** *"No, no! I don't believe you! Midas is in that room! I want to see him!"*
>
> *Six-year-old Jimmy collapses onto the floor, crying, kicking, and flailing his arms.*
>
> **Parent:** *(still standing) "You can't see him, Jimmy. Midas is gone."*
>
> **Jimmy:** *(screaming loudly) "He is not gone! You're lying! I want my Midas!"*

What's Going on Here?

Children grieve just as deeply as adults. However, until children reach the ages of eight or nine, most do not possess the ability to think rationally about, or verbally express, their needs and feelings of grief. Thus, many children act out grief through playing games, drawing pictures, and even misbehaving. Expressions of anger and irritability, like Jimmy's tantrums, are often due to children's feelings of confusion, insecurity, and loss of control.

How Can I Help?

Cases involving children are tricky. Some parents are touchy and don't appreciate any interference in terms of how they raise their kids. Your well-meaning suggestions about how to deal with children's grief may put some parents on the defensive, especially if they think you are criticizing their values or parenting styles.

However, most parents sincerely want to help their children and will be open to your ideas if you approach them in a gentle way. This is a good time to use acknowledging and normalizing. This lets parents know you recognize that they want to be responsible, protective parents. If you

have children yourself, you can also use self-disclosure, briefly relating the methods you used to help your own children deal with pet loss.

When it comes to cases involving kids, though, the most helpful effort you can make is to try to help educate. Enlighten parents about the facts pertaining to children and grief. Remember, most people operate from a host of misconceptions about grief. When parents are uninformed about grief, they can inadvertently cause their children to experience more emotional harm.

If you're not comfortable educating parents about the needs of children during pet loss, refer them to a professional grief counselor or make books and videotapes available to them. (See the Resources section at the back of this book.)

If the situation requires immediate intervention, like the scenario at the beginning of this situation, use touch, direct eye contact, and attending behaviors to calm the child, active listening to really hear what the child is asking for, and then, as much as you can, advocate for the child's needs to be met.

To be honest, this may require some additional time and effort on your part. For example, if a companion animal has been killed by a car and is cut, bloody, or disfigured in some way, you may need to take time to clean the blood away, bandage a wound, or, at least, remove the medical equipment you were using to try to save the animal's life. Then, after preparing the child with a description of the wounds and/or physical changes he or she is likely to see, you may need to accompany the child as the final viewing and last good-byes take place. With preparation, viewing a pet's body is almost always helpful to a child because it helps him accept the reality of the pet's death.

Being an instrumental part of teaching children how to face death and grief is the epitome of providing client support. There is simply nothing more satisfying. If you're successful, you'll help create a more emotionally healthy child and a more positive experience with veterinary medicine for the child to remember.

Other ways to support parents and children are to:

- Encourage parents to be honest with children. Parents don't lie to children because they are malicious, but because they think a lie might protect their child from further pain. Yet, lies create confusion and mistrust. If parents ask you to lie, take that as a plea for help, gently decline to do so, and offer to assist parents in telling their children the truth.

- Encourage parents to include children in decision-making and to trust and honor their children's requests. With preparation and support, children benefit from making their own decisions and facing their own fears. If children want to attend their pets' euthanasias or view their pets' bodies after death, it is usually better to allow it than to deprive them of a way to meet a deeply felt need.

- Avoid using euphemisms and clichés like put to sleep and gone to heaven. Young children take what adults say literally. If they think their pet is sleeping, they also think it will soon wake up. For young children, associating going to sleep with never waking up can be a scary thought.

Keep in Mind

- The experience of pet loss is *not* a dress rehearsal for children. The loss is just as significant as the loss of a human family member. It should be acknowledged and not trivialized.

- Children grieve just as intensely as adults, but they do so more sporadically due to their shorter attention spans. Even during an actual owner-present euthanasia (which even young children can attend as long as they've been prepared and allowed to make the decision about attending), young children may cry one minute and ask if they can play outdoors the next.

Quick Tips

What to Say, What to Do

- Before you intervene, remind yourself to be kind, respectful, and non-judgmental. Don't take sides, and be sure your voice doesn't have a scolding tone.

- Use touch and eye contact to gain both the parent's and Jimmy's attention. You may need to squat down to be on Jimmy's eye level.

- Speak slowly and softly. You might say, "Jimmy, Mrs. Smith, I can see how sad and difficult this is for both of you."

- Structure the environment. Get them some privacy. If necessary, take Jimmy's hand. Guide the parent by placing your hand on her arm or even putting your arm around her shoulders as you lead them toward a private area. You might say, "I'd like you both to come with me to a room where we can talk about Midas and decide what we can do to help you say good-bye to him. Jimmy, I promise we won't move Midas until we've all decided what to do."

- Educate the parent about children and grief.

- Facilitate a consensus regarding how everyone involved can best have their needs met.

- Children want and deserve to be told the truth about their pets' deaths. Lies do not protect children; they create confusion and feelings of mistrust.

- Children want and deserve to be included in decisions concerning their pets' treatment, euthanasia, and body care. They also benefit from opportunities to say good-bye. With parental support, children can view their pets' bodies after death and attend their pets' memorial services.

- Most children need time to grieve for their pets who have died and do not want to immediately adopt another one. Presenting children with new pets too soon gives them the impression that loved ones who die aren't unique and special and are easily replaced.

How Will I Know if I've Been Successful?

When the family returns to your practice with a new pet, you will know they appreciated your sensitivity and assistance during the death of their former companion animal. Children often hold veterinary professionals responsible for their pets' deaths. When this happens, they influence their parents' choice of veterinarian by resisting any future interactions with you. When you walk the fine line between supporting children's needs to be involved and parents' needs to protect them, you develop loyal, grateful clients—no matter what their ages.

My Notes

Figure 5
The Hallmark Characteristics
of Grief in Children

- Babies (birth to 1 year) respond to grief by crying, withdrawing, clinging, and even regressing developmentally, but they are not aware of the cause of the increased tension. Babies need to be reassured, cuddled, and kept to their usual routines as much as possible.

- Toddlers and pre-schoolers (2 to 4 years) do not understand that death is permanent. They often ask when their pet is coming back. Toddlers are curious and relaxed about death and ask lots of questions. They often grieve by play-acting, acting out, and misbehaving. If they do not find outlets for grief, they may develop psychosomatic complaints like stomachaches. Like babies, toddlers need to be reassured and kept to their routines as much as possible. They also benefit from outlets like imaginative play or drawing pictures as ways to express their grief.

- School-aged children (5 to 12 years) are usually conditioned to the prevailing cultural and familial views and taboos that surround death. Some fear death. Others taunt it, believing they can hide, run away, or control death like they see superheros do on TV. Most younger school-agers grieve in ways similar to toddlers; however, around the age of eight, they gain a cognitive understanding of death and realize it is both permanent and universal. School-aged children are helped when adults provide opportunities for them to talk and to ask questions about death. They also benefit from seeing adults openly and honestly expressing their feelings of grief.

- Adolescents (13 to 17 years) are unpredictable, self-conscious, and prone to mood swings. Their grief responses are often confusing and contradictory. Adolescents need opportunities to express their grief verbally, so they do not develop psychosomatic complaints or complicate grief with unresolved feelings of guilt and anger. Adults need to create opportunities for adolescents to talk about grief. They also benefit by actively participating in decisions and after-death arrangements like funeral planning.

- Young adults (18 to 21 years) often view the death of their childhood pet as a rite of passage—the passage of their own childhood. They may feel guilty for abandoning their companion animal when they left home and resentful if they were not included in decisions regarding treatment and/or euthanasia. Like adolescents, young adults benefit from open discussion as well as active and equal participation.

Situation 8
Helping Seniors

> **Senior Client:** *"I have no one to help me with Toby's body. Would you come to my place and bury him for me?"*

What's Going on Here?

As people age, their physical strength and stamina decline, making older people incapable of undertaking all the activities they did in younger days. Memory losses due to aging or disease can also occur. Retirement may bring a change in standard of living. Older people living on fixed incomes may not be able to afford treatments for their pets and may be forced to make life and death decisions based on finances. Due to these factors, older people may need extra support, time, care, and understanding when their pets are ill or have died.

Another concern about older people is that they may have lost the majority of their emotional support network. Spouses and friends may have died and children and other relatives may live far away. To help them fill in the gaps, you can keep a reference list of resources in your community for senior citizens. This could include transportation services, drug and pet stores which may offer senior discounts, and human service agencies or volunteers who are willing to assist seniors with unexpected needs like burying a cat or dog.

How Can I Help?

Demographers tell us that our population is aging, so you can expect an increasing number of your clients to be in the over-65 age group. When you deal with older people, you sometimes need to repeat information several times because clients may be hard-of-hearing or may need extra time to understand what is being said. It may also be helpful for you to write out information or instructions, as elderly people may not be able to remember detailed information once they leave your clinic. An older person living alone may want to call a relative or friend to help them make a decision about the pet's care.

As you work with older clients, you may find that it is common for them to reminisce about the past. They may tell you about other pets or family members who have died. Discussions may also bring up comments about their own health or the acknowledgment that their own lives are drawing to a close. Don't trivialize the importance of these feelings. A response like "Oh, Ruth, you'll live forever" is not helpful. An open, honest discussion of death may provide an older person with an important but rare opportunity to tell someone how they feel about aging and dying. While these conversations may sound morose, they are actually comforting and helpful to older people. Instead of changing the subject, try saying something like, "Well, Ruth, when you do die—and I hope it's not for a very long time—I will miss you."

Keep in Mind

- For older pet owners, companion animals are often symbolically linked with deceased loved ones. Perhaps the dog who is now dying was an anniversary present from a spouse who has died, or the elderly cat may have belonged to a deceased sibling. It is likely that most older people have not fully grieved all of their losses. Thus, when older people are faced with the deaths of companion animals, it is likely that some unresolved grief will be triggered, as well as possible fears and anxieties about their own deaths.

- Due to generational differences and the social climate in which they were raised, elderly pet owners may have more discomfort with the open expression of emotion than younger clients.

- Elderly owners may have had numerous experiences with pet death, companion animal euthanasia, and viewing bodies over the years. Unfortunately, those situations may have been poorly handled, leaving elderly owners skeptical about your offers to provide grief support. In these cases, their current decisions (to not be present at euthanasia, to not view their pet's body) may be based on outdated information and previous negative experiences. With gentle persistence and education, you may be able to give them a new, much more positive experience with pet loss.

- Respect the years of learning that elderly people have, and remember that they are all individuals with their own levels of education, life experiences, and mental and physical competencies. Don't assume older clients need special consideration until you have asked them directly or observed a decline in their functioning for yourself.

How Will I Know if I've Been Successful?

Companion animals have a positive effect on the physical and emotional well-being of older people. In fact, research into the relationships between pets and the elderly has been so persuasive that laws are beginning to change nationally to allow elderly pet owners to keep pets in retirement centers, nursing homes, and federally funded public housing.

If pets provide significant health benefits for older people, the deaths of their pets most likely affect their health as well. Check in with your older clients as often as you can after they've lost a pet. While replacing a pet is not an effective remedy for grief, there are so many benefits of pet ownership for seniors that, in this case, it may be an effective solution. Encourage your older clients to adopt a new animal. Help them select one that fits their lifestyle and physical capabilities. Make it easy for them to provide medical care for their pet. Offer senior discounts and even house calls. Finally, if your client is hesitant to adopt another pet because she is afraid the pet may outlive her, help her devise a plan designating who would adopt and care for her pet after her own death.

My Notes

Quick Tips

What to Say, What to Do

- Acknowledge the emotional dilemma underlying your client's request. You might say, "It sounds like taking care of Toby's body might be difficult for you to do alone."

- Educate your client about other available body care options, like cremation or burial at a pet cemetery.

- Decide if you can be of direct support (help bury the dog yourself) or indirect support (facilitate the process of finding someone else to help your client bury her dog). You might say, "Ruth, I would be happy to help you bury Toby, but it will have to be during a time when I am not needed here at the clinic," or "Ruth, I myself can't help you bury Toby, but I'm sure I can help you find someone who can."

- Ask tough questions in order to determine which resource is best equipped to help your client. Ask her, "Which relative (or friend or neighbor) would you like me to call and ask to help you with Toby?"

- If questions and assessment of your client's support system fail to reveal a helper, contact your client's church, or a human service, or volunteer agency. It may take a bit longer for them to identify a willing volunteer, but with persistence, they are usually successful.

Situation 9
Client Guilt

> **Client:** *"Oh, I knew I should have fixed our gate! It didn't latch right, and Snoopy got out, and now he's dead. I killed him! As sure as if I had been driving that car myself, I'm the one who caused his death. I will never, ever forgive myself."*

What's Going on Here?

Guilt is the critic, the inner voice that judges thoughts, actions, behaviors, decisions, and feelings. Sometimes guilt is justified and other times it is not. For instance, some clients do create the circumstances that either directly or indirectly cause their pet's death. They may be negligent in how they care for their companion animals, or they may knowingly take part in a potentially dangerous situation, like allowing a pet to ride in the open bed of a pick-up truck. When death occurs in these cases, feelings of guilt may be justified.

Other guilt isn't justified. For example, many clients feel guilty when their pets are diagnosed with a terminal illness. They feel they could have done something to prevent the disease or at least noticed the pet's symptoms sooner. In addition, many clients feel guilty after euthanizing their pets, even if the decision was clearly in the animal's best interests.

In general, guilt probably stems from an owner's belief that they have breached the contract they made with their pet to keep the pet alive, safe, and healthy. The support you offer clients who feel guilty varies according to whether or not your client's guilt is justified.

How Can I Help?

Even when guilt is not justified, it is just as difficult to make guilty feelings go away. No matter what you say, some clients will remain convinced that the little, insignificant things they did or didn't do actually caused their companion animals' deaths. Clients hang on to these beliefs and their guilt for a multitude of reasons, none of which are within the scope of your abilities or responsibilities to resolve. The best you can do to support a client dealing with unjustified guilt is to patiently and repeatedly review the medical facts pertaining to his pet's death and acknowledge his guilty feelings.

Occasionally, you will see clients who deserve to feel guilty. Perhaps they have been grossly negligent or even abusive to their pets. In these cases, your goal is not to alleviate your client's guilt, but to act as an advocate for the animal. In most instances, these are not the kinds of clients you want to cultivate. Rather, they are the ones you want to report to the authorities and hopefully prevent from owning other animals in the future.

How Will I Know if I've Been Successful?

Most clients who feel guilty also feel embarrassed that they may have harmed their pets by making bad decisions or participating in dangerous activities. Along with their embarrassment, they are probably also wondering how their pet's accidental injury or death has affected your opinion of them. If you can separate the person from their questionable behavior, you can probably honestly say something like, "Mark, I can see that this mistake is making you feel terribly guilty. However, I believe you are a responsible and conscientious pet owner who never intended to bring any harm to Snoopy. I know you've learned a lesson from this experience."

This statement won't do much to alleviate your client's guilt, but it will reassure him that you still support him, won't judge him, and don't wish to see him punish himself over the accident. He will return your kindness and understanding by remaining a loyal client—and by fixing the latch on his gate.

My Notes

Quick Tips

What to Say, What to Do

- Acknowledge your client's feelings of guilt and create an opportunity for him to talk about his feelings. You can't change or fix another person's guilty feelings. You can only listen without judgment. For example, in the case scenario that opens this situation, instead of saying "Don't feel so bad," or "It wasn't really your fault," you might say something like, "I hear how guilty you feel about Snoopy's death, Mark, and I know you would give anything to be able to go back in time and fix that gate."

- Structure the environment so you and your client can have a private, emotional conversation. During the conversation, use attending behaviors, touch, active listening, and paraphrasing in such comments as, "Sounds as though you had every intention of fixing your gate," and "If I'm hearing you right, Snoopy had never gotten out of your yard before."

- Facilitate a way for your client to say good-bye to his dog or even to apologize to Snoopy for indirectly causing the accident. You might suggest that your client view his pet's body, go home and write a letter to his pet, or compensate for his negligence by donating to or volunteering with an animal-related organization.

- The guilt that is commonly present when clients decide to euthanize a very sick or injured pet can't be taken away completely, but it can be minimized. You can gently tell clients that people often use guilt to distract themselves from the more painful feelings of sadness and loneliness. You can also give them permission to experience the full range of grief manifestations that accompany loss. Finally, you can remind clients that you consider euthanasia to be a privilege and a gift and say something like, "You did everything of a medical nature that you could possibly do for Snoopy and, in the end, you gave him a loving gift—a peaceful, painless death."

Situation 10
Body Care

> *Berkley, a nine-year-old yellow lab, underwent exploratory surgery. During surgery, Berkley was found to have cancer all through his abdomen. The veterinarian contacted his clients. Together, they decided to euthanize Berkley while he was still anesthetized. The owners told the veterinarian that they would like to have their dog's body back for burial.*
>
> *Thinking that his clients would probably not want to see their pet dead, the veterinarian placed Berkley in a large, black plastic bag and sealed it tightly with a twist tie. When the clients arrived an hour later to pick up Berkley's body, they were confused. They believed their dog had been too big to fit into the bag that was lying in front of them on the floor of the examination room. Reluctantly, they removed the tie and looked inside. From their perspective, they saw what had been their big, cuddly dog stuffed into a garbage bag, contorted into a grotesque posture. Crying, the clients left without even talking to the veterinarian.*
>
> *When the veterinarian was told that his clients had left abruptly, he felt confused and a bit angry. He had done his best for their dog and handled the body in the way he thought they would want. He didn't understand their reaction.*

What's Going on Here?

The matter of body care is a delicate issue in terms of the client/veterinary professional relationship. Since many owners have invested lots of years, money, and love in the physical care of their companion animals, their pets' bodies remain important to them even after death. When clients perceive that their pets' bodies have not been treated with respect and reverence, their grief can become complicated, and your relationship can be severely jeopardized.

How Can I Help?

Whenever possible, decisions about body care should be made prior to the death of a companion animal. Offer owners all of the body care options that are available to them and explain each honestly and sensitively. The cost of each option should also be disclosed. It is helpful to use visual aids during this explanation. For example, if your practice is able to make caskets or urns available for owners to purchase, samples can be shown. You can also offer to show your clients what the cremains of a dog or a cat look like. Many people think cremains are like the gray, papery ashes that remain in a fireplace after a log has been burned, but they are actually more like sand or small pebbles, often with larger chips of bone included.

Explain body care options in a private area. Use a conversational, quiet voice and respond to your clients' tears or questions with touch, attending behaviors, and honesty.

When discussing body care options, you might say something like, "Marge, I can offer you three options for taking care of Berkley's body after he dies. The first option is to take him with you and bury him in a pet cemetery or in an appropriate place on your own property. If that is your choice, we encourage you to bring something like a blanket or a nice box from home to transport his body in because our options here are limited to large plastic bags or vinyl caskets that cost between thirty and fifty dollars. Second, you can cremate Berkley's body and either keep his cremains, dispose of them yourself, or ask the crematory to dispose of them for you. If you want the crematory to return them to you, and you decide to keep them rather than scatter them outdoors, you may want to choose an urn or another kind of container to keep them in. Cremation has become a popular and practical body care option for pets because so many people in our society move quite often. This way, they can always take their pets with them. Your third option, Marge, is to have us take care of Berkley's body for you. Although I wish I had a more pleasing option to offer you, my only option is [mass incineration, mass burial at the local landfill, or delivery to a rendering company—fill in the blank with whatever is accurate]."

Since the majority of mass burials take place in landfills, owners should be given this information. While it might not matter to some of your clients, the thought of burying their companion animals at a landfill might be quite distasteful for others.

One very important and often overlooked aspect of body care concerns remains retrieval. Remains retrieval refers to the time when clients return to your office to either pick up their pet's body or cremated remains. Clients often have expectations about how this event will be handled only to experience something completely different. For example, when retrieving remains, some clients want to take

time to sit down and talk with one or more of the veterinary professionals who helped them when their pet died. Another client will prefer to simply pick up the pet's body or cremains without seeing anyone. Regardless of how clients want the event structured, a warm expression of condolence and support should be provided by whoever delivers the pet's body or cremains to the client.

If clients wish to schedule an appointment for remains retrieval, it is important to set a time for an office visit. Given the sensitive nature of this meeting, it is probably best to not charge clients for this appointment. When clients arrive, it is helpful to take them into a private room—your office, an exam room, or the visitation/euthanasia room—and gently present the pet's body or cremains to them. If possible, don't use the same room where the client's pet died or was euthanized. If clients are picking up their pet's body, prepare them for what they will see and feel and have the body positioned so it is pleasing to look at and ready to transport. If clients are picking up their pet's cremains, you should also prepare them for what they will see and feel. For many owners, the difference in form, size, volume, and weight between a furry body and a container of cremains can be shocking and emotionally overwhelming.

Keep in Mind

- If you and your clients know about a pet's death prior to their retrieving the remains, ask them to bring something from home in which they can wrap or transport their pet's body. Then, you can be certain that your client will feel the item used is appropriate.

- If you are keeping the animal's body in a cooler until other family members can view it or pick it up, curl the body into a sleep-like position so owners will be able to place the body in a casket or easily transport it in their car. For this reason, it's a good idea to keep a box, a vinyl casket, or another container at your clinic for shaping and storage purposes.

- If an owner is taking a pet's body home, be sure the animal's body is not carried out to the owner's car through your busy waiting room.

- There are times when it may be desirable to perform necropsies on animals who have died. Where necropsy is warranted, the option must be tactfully introduced and explained to clients. Several points are relevant to tactful discussions of necropsy.

    1) Most pet owners are unfamiliar with the term necropsy and have more understanding of the term postmortem examination.

    2) Cosmetic necropsies, where only selected tissues are removed, are usually recommended when an owner wants to find out why the companion animal died, but also want the pet's body returned to him for burial.

    3) Whether a necropsy is complete or cosmetic, it should never be performed without an owner's knowledge or permission.

- Body care options also need to be explained to children. It's helpful to draw pictures and use appropriate props like caskets, urns, and cremains to explain the concepts to kids. Think ahead about how you will explain body care options like burial and cremation to children.

How Will I Know if I've Been Successful?

Body care is a sensitive issue. It is also an area where it's tempting to judge your clients' body care decisions. For example, there are pet owners who choose to have their horses cremated at a cost of over $1,000, to bury their companion animals in expensive, human caskets, and even hire taxidermists to preserve their pets' bodies so they retain the same appearance after death that they had in life. When it comes to body care, the measure of success is not whether or not your clients make the body care decision that you believe is right, practical, moral, or even sane. Rather, success is achieved when you facilitate honest, open, nonjudgmental discussions about body care and help your clients arrive at decisions that are right for them. These are the body care decisions that bring both you and your clients peace of mind.

My Notes

Situation 11
After-death Follow Up

Dear John, Jill, and Meghan,

I have thought of you so often since CeeCee died. I want you to know that I believe your decision to help her die was the right one. Her cancer had advanced to the point that her quality of life was greatly diminished, and she just wasn't enjoying life much anymore. During treatment, you did everything you could for her and, in the end, spared her any further pain and suffering. Our staff made a donation to the local humane society in CeeCee's name. I remember you said you adopted her there twelve years ago. I've also enclosed CeeCee's collar for you. I believe it can be comforting to keep familiar mementos from our pets' lives.

The next few days and weeks are bound to be sad for you all. I'll check in with you next week to see how you're doing and to find out if we can be of any further support to you.

Sincerely,
Jean Wills, DVM

What's Going on Here?

Contemporary veterinary professionals realize that making condolences and creating memorials are part of the normal grieving and helping processes. Thus, reaching out to clients after their pets die via the mail, telephone, or in person is not only a sign of compassion, it is also a wise business practice. For one reason or another, a significant number of clients don't return to a veterinary practice after their pets die. In fact, many pet owners find it is just too painful for them to again face the people—and even the building—where they last saw their pet alive. However, a friendly, concerned contact after the death of a pet can break through this avoidance and denial aspect of grief, assure clients that you understand their loss, and can be of support.

Clinical experience proves that pet owners would rather have veterinary medical professionals talk about a pet who died rather than pretend that nothing ever happened. Therefore, the vast majority of pet owners do not view condolences and memorials as morbid, intrusive, silly, or overly sentimental. They view them as sensitive ways for you to honor the deep, special bond they shared with their companion animal.

How Can I Help?

Condolence cards and telephone calls should be sent or made as soon after a pet's death as possible. Whether you're writing or speaking the words, let your clients know that you are addressing their loss by recalling something unique about their pet and referring to it in specific terms. For example, you might say, "I'll always remember CeeCee's beautiful blue eyes and the long, loving looks she gave me." This reassures clients that you are reaching out to them personally and not treating their case as just another statistic.

While you are offering your condolences, you can also invite clients to contact you if they have further questions or concerns and take advantage of the opportunity to educate clients about normal grief. If you're sending your condolences, you can include printed grief education materials and referrals to local pet loss support groups or pet loss counselors.

Just as there are many ways to offer your condolences to clients, there are also many ways you can help clients memorialize their pets. For instance, you can send flowers or make donations to animal organizations or to special service groups in the names of your clients' pets. You can also give clients permission to create their own memorials. Many pet owners collect their memories into scrapbooks, photo albums, or on videotape.

For some pet owners, it is meaningful to have an object that links them to their pets. This object may be a dog's collar, a cat's toy mouse, a special blanket, or even a food dish. The object may also be part of the actual animal, such as a feather, the wool of a llama, part of a horse's mane or tail, or even a paw print set in clay. Tell clients that, if these objects comfort them, they should keep them with them or in plain view in their homes.

Many clients also choose to conduct funerals or memorial services for their pets. Some funerals are simple, private ceremonies. Others are elaborate, public good-bye rituals, complete with caskets and graveside services. Sometimes clients invite their veterinarians to their pets' funerals. You may want to attend some of these as a way for you to say good-bye to a special patient. This may be particularly true if you are conducting a home euthanasia. Whether or not you choose to attend them is up to you. Accept your clients' invitations with caution, though, as attending every funeral or memorial service can become exhausting and time-consuming.

How Will I Know if I've Been Successful?

There are two actions that will tell you your clients appreciate receiving your condolences and memorials. They will call or write you to say thank you, and they will return to your practice when they need veterinary care. In short, your professional relationship will continue with an even deeper feeling of mutual care and loyalty.

Quick Tips

What to Say, What to Do

- Acknowledge your client's loss and offer your support and condolences either by telephone or by mail within a few days of the pet's death.

- Verbally acknowledge the pet's death during the first face-to-face, post-death contact you have with your client, even if this is several months after the death in a public place like the grocery store. Use direct eye contact, a quiet voice, touch (if it seems appropriate), and say something like, "Hello, Jill. I haven't seen you since CeeCee died. How have you and your family been since then?"

- If your client begins to cry at the mention of her pet's name, normalize her tears, and give her permission to cry and to talk about her pet and her feelings of grief.

- Attend, paraphrase, listen actively, and, if appropriate, self-disclose about your own need to talk and to cry after a pet you loved died. Encourage your client to find a way to memorialize her pet if she hasn't already done so.

- If your condolence conversation is taking place in a public area (e.g., the grocery store or your clinic's waiting room), structure the environment and invite your client to join you in a more private place (e.g., a coffee shop, an examination room or office). You might say, "Jill, it sounds like it might feel good for you to talk a bit about CeeCee, and I'd like to hear more about how you've been . Do you have time for a cup of coffee over in the deli?"

My Notes

Situation 12
Other Pets' Grief

> **Client:** *"My surviving dog, Nellie, has been acting strange ever since my golden retriever, Mack, died. She won't eat or drink unless I stand right next to her, and she's torn up the carpet in every entryway of our house. Is it possible she's grieving for Mack?"*

What's Going on Here?

Animals in the same household often develop strong bonds with one another and, when separated, can exhibit stress reactions like the ones described above. The grief responses of companion animals have not been scientifically studied, but dozens of anecdotes describing surviving pets' grief have been reported.

How Can I Help?

There isn't much scientific, or even clinical, documentation regarding how you can best provide support to owners who are dealing with their surviving pets' grief. The first effort you can make, though, is to acknowledge and normalize your clients' concerns regarding their surviving pets' behavior. Some clients feel foolish when they assign human characteristics to their animals. Therefore, they are likely to find your validation of their observations very supportive.

Based on what is known about separation reactions and animal behavior, some logical assumptions about modifying or minimizing an animal's negative behaviors can be made. In terms of actual client support strategies, you can educate clients about pertinent animal behaviors, like separation anxiety, and make the following three suggestions. If the problems are serious, you may want to refer clients to a certified animal behaviorist or to a qualified animal trainer.

1. Keep daily routines the same. Animals usually respond to environments that are predictable, familiar, and consistent.

2. Do not inadvertently reinforce or reward negative behavior changes. For example, if a pet learns that anxious pacing results in repeated invitations to join its owner for a snuggle on the forbidden couch, it may be more likely to continue the anxious behavior. If the owner introduced in the case described at the beginning of this helping strategy continues to stand patiently beside her dog while she eats, she'll create a great deal of anxiety for both of them surrounding mealtime. Instead of reinforcing unwanted behaviors, owners should provide their pets with positive reinforcement, such as attention and affection, when their pets are behaving in desirable ways.

3. Watch for changes in the dominance hierarchy when there are two or more surviving pets. This is particularly true if the pet who died was the dominant animal because the remaining animals often compete for the dominant spot in the pecking order. Competition may involve growling, hissing, and even fighting, but the attacks usually do not result in injury. For the most part, owners should not punish their animals, but let the animals end the skirmishes on their own.

Keep in Mind

- A great deal of anecdotal evidence points to the fact that animals do grieve for one another.

- Many of the grief symptoms displayed by companion animals seem similar to those of human grief. However, there can also be a complete absence of symptoms following another pet's death. For this reason and others, the separation reaction in animals can not be exactly equated to that in humans.

- Behavioral changes in animals may be reactions to their owner's grief.
- Adopting a new friend for the surviving pet usually backfires. There is no guarantee that any two animals will form close, friendly relationships.

How Will I Know if I've Been Successful?

Owners sometimes want to let their surviving pets see and even smell the body of a pet who has died. In fact, some owners even want to bring their surviving pets to their dying animal's euthanasia. While there is no scientific evidence that this has any affect on surviving animals, it is sometimes helpful to the owners. If owners feel strongly about involving their pets in this way, it is helpful to give them permission to do so. Requests like this measure your success at providing grief support because owners trust and feel comfortable enough with you to take a risk on behalf of their companion animals.

My Notes

Quick Tips

What to Say, What to Do

- Acknowledge that animals do grieve for one another, and acknowledge your client's concern for her surviving pet by saying something like, "I think it's very possible that Nellie misses Mack. I'm sure it's difficult for you to see Nellie so lonely and upset all the time."

- Normalize your client's concerns. Use self-disclosure if you've experienced a similar situation by saying something like, "You know, many of our clients tell us about situations similar to yours. When my dog Celia died, my other dog, Millie, went through the same kind of adjustment you're describing."

- Educate about animal behavior, especially pack behavior and separation anxiety.

- If appropriate, refer to a certified animal behaviorist or qualified trainer.

Figure 6
The Hallmark Characteristics of Grief in Companion Animals

- Anxiety, restlessness, or a need to stay close to the owner
- Changes in eating, drinking, sleeping, or exercise habits
- Depression, heavy sighing, or disinterest in usual activities
- Destructive behaviors
- High-pitched distress vocalizations (especially in young animals)
- Housesoiling
- Searching the yard, house, and other familiar areas for the animal that has died

Situation 13
Adopting New Pets

> **Client:** *"I'm going out today to get a huge, gray tomcat who looks just like Jitters and I'm going to name him Jitters Jr."*

What's Going on Here?

After a companion animal dies, most pet owners have one of three basic reactions to beginning again with a new companion animal: 1) They vow to never again own another pet, 2) they vow to adopt a new pet as soon as possible, or 3) they resign themselves to a period of grieving before they adopt a new pet but then feel guilty when they do adopt and realize how much they love their new companion animal. In the last case, many pet owners believe that a deep new bond diminishes the bond they shared with their former pet.

Pet owners who immediately adopt new pets are usually trying to avoid the sadness and loneliness of grief. Comments like the one above should alert you to the possibility that clients may be trying to bring their pet back in the form of an outwardly identical new companion animal.

How Can I Help?

In some cases, it may be appropriate for a client to adopt a new pet fairly soon. For example, some pet owners experience long periods of anticipatory grief prior to their pet's death and feel ready to again share their lives with a companion animal. Also, pet owners who are blind, deaf, or disabled often quickly adopt new service animals to meet their immediate needs.

However, as a general rule, it's a good idea to caution your clients about adopting a new pet too soon. Educate your clients about the fact that animals are as individual as people and have different personalities, habits, and needs. Tell them that, in most cases, the new pet is nothing like the one who died.

For example, even though the two pets may be of the same gender and breed, the pet that died may have been older and more mellow in tem-

perament, while the new pet might be young and untrained. While clients may have thought of the pet that died as a confidante and protector, the new pet may seem more like an unruly, needy child. When pet owners expect one thing from a companion animal, but get another, they often fail to form adequate bonds. Then, on top of grief, they feel guilt, especially if they decide they cannot provide the new pet with a loving home. Use your skills to help clients think through the consequences of a decision they may make in haste.

At the other end of the spectrum are clients who make comments like, "I'll never get another cat. It's just too hard on me to lose them. Besides, I could never love another animal as much as I loved Jitters." Your first reaction to a comment like this is probably to say something like, "Oh, you don't mean that! Think of all the animals out there who need good homes. The best thing for you right now would be to go out and adopt a new kitten." However, this advice is almost never helpful. The replacement philosophy that commonly surrounds the death of a pet implies that companion animal death is a relatively insignificant loss and that pets are easily replaced. In addition, giving advice, as opposed to active listening, tends to discount clients' feelings and stop further conversation.

When clients say they'll never own another pet, most don't really mean it. Rather, the comment reflects the grief they feel about this pet's death. If you acknowledge and validate your clients' feelings instead of trying to convince or persuade them to feel otherwise, you'll provide more effective support. It's usually more effective to simply paraphrase your clients' comments, saying something like, "It sounds like this loss is especially sad for you," or "I can hear that the thought of a new pet is not very comforting right now."

In the final scenario, it is not uncommon for pet owners to feel guilty once they have adopted a new pet and realize that they love it as much as they loved the one that died. Intense feelings for new pets often make clients feel they are being disloyal to the pet that has died. This time of simultaneously letting go and starting over can make some pet owners wonder how their former companion animals can so easily be replaced in their hearts. You can help clients sort through their loyalty conflicts by letting them know that love is unlimited and that human beings are capable of loving more than one being at the same time, both living and dead. Clients also need to understand that they do not have to make a choice between loving either their new pet or the pet that died. Instead, they can choose to love them both, in slightly different ways.

How Will I Know if I've Been Successful?

When grief progresses normally, your clients will begin to talk about getting a new pet. They will make comments like, "I miss having a dog in my house," or "I've always been intrigued with schnauzers. I might try that breed this time." Comments like these imply an interest in, rather than a desperate need for, a new pet. They tell you that clients have reached a stronger, more confident place in their grief and are now ready to explore the possibility of adopting a new pet. At this point, you can give them permission to begin again and refer them to the nearest reputable breeder or humane society shelter.

My Notes

Quick Tips

What to Say, What to Do

- Acknowledge the loss that has just occurred by saying something like, "Jitters meant so much to you. I know his loss has been very difficult."

- Educate about normal symptoms of grief and effective helpful strategies by saying something like, "During grief, it's normal to feel anxious and restless. In fact, many people think that the sooner they adopt a new pet, the sooner they'll get over grieving for the one that just died. Yet, most often, it just doesn't work that way. I wonder if you need to give yourself a bit of time to grieve for Jitters before you adopt Jitters Jr.?"

- Facilitate decisions surrounding adopting a new pet by saying something like, "Jitters was an older cat, wise to your routines and house rules. Have you thought about what it might be like to get a new cat just now?"

- Depending on how you feel about the owner's decision, validate the reasoning behind it and give permission to adopt a new pet. You might say, "After talking with you today, it sounds as though you're ready to adopt a new pet. I'll be anxious to meet the newest member of your family.

Situation 14
Making Referrals to Grief Counselors and Pet Loss Support Groups

> **Client:** *"My daughter died three years ago, and Betsy was her cat. She laid on her bed right beside her every day while she was sick. Losing Betsy is like losing Janie all over again. I don't think I'll be able to bear the grief again."*

What's Going on Here?

The death of this client's cat represents what is called a symbolic loss. A symbolic loss is one that is associated with a previous loss in life. A companion animal may represent a pet owner's last link to a special person, place, thing, or time in life. The pet's death, then, physically destroys that link. Although pet loss is a significant loss in its own right, the grief a pet owner feels may be greater when an old loss is also triggered. Symbolic losses are often more intense, may last longer, and may be reactivated more easily than nonsymbolic losses.

There are many ways to make professional support available to clients. However, even if professional support exists, it won't be of help if you are uncomfortable making referrals. It is useful for you to have some stock phrases you can use to let clients know about the human service resources that are available. A sampling of some classic referral techniques and statements follow. Be sure to pair these words with nonverbal helping techniques like touch, direct eye contact, and other attending behaviors.

How Can I Help?

It's not possible for you to meet your clients' needs for ongoing grief education and support, so you may need to refer some of them to a professional grief therapist or pet loss support group. There are several effective ways to do this. For instance, you can provide every client who experiences pet loss with a packet of written materials describing local support groups, pet loss counselors, and pet loss support hot lines. With referral names, addresses, and telephone numbers in hand, clients are made aware of the resources available to them and can choose for themselves which, if any, they want to use.

Another way you can make a referral is on a case-by-case basis. You can assess which of your clients may be in need of extended support by examining several factors. These factors may include the strength of your client's human-companion animal bond, the circumstances surrounding the companion animal's death, your client's personal support system, and your client's own ability to cope. When one or more of these factors seem to be deficient, the client is probably a good candidate for referral.

Keep in Mind

- The Delta Society offers a state-by-state directory of pet loss support groups. They also offer a packet of materials describing how to set up a support group in your community. See the Resources section for more information.

- Not all mental health professionals understand or are skilled in working with issues of grief. Likewise, not all grief counselors are sympathetic to issues of pet loss and pet owner grief. If you are interested in teaming up with a mental health professional, it is important to screen your potential candidates and to choose wisely.

- If you do not have access to a pet loss support group, there are several pet loss support hot lines that your clients can call. These are staffed by trained, paraprofessional volunteers. The telephone numbers of several pet loss support hot lines are listed in Resources.

How Will I Know if I've Been Successful?

You may have to refer clients to a human service professional or pet loss support group several times before they are ready to actually talk with one. For many people, there is a stigma attached to talking to a counselor. Thus, they avoid the encounter for as long as possible. However, clients who are reluctant to seek professional help are often the ones who continue to ask you to help them with their grief. It's important for you to continue to abide by the principles of your paraprofessional helping role. This means you need to sensitively, but consistently, decline to provide them with further help and refer them to the counselor with whom you work, regardless of whether or not they actually seek help.

My Notes

Quick Tips

What to Say, What to Do

- Self-disclose by saying something like, "I know how hard Betsy's death is for you. I work with a person who specializes in helping pet owners deal with the grief they feel after their pets die, especially in a situation like yours where there is a connection between Betsy and Janie. Many of my clients talk with her at least once, and it seems to help a great deal. I talk with her about cases that are tough for me, too. I'd like to give you her name and number."

- Normalize your client's grief by saying something like, "It sounds as though the connection between Janie and Betsy's deaths is complicating your grief. This is common and quite normal. I know your feelings can be sorted out, but I'm simply not trained in this area. I would be doing you a disservice if I tried to be the one who helped you work through them. I do know someone who can help you, though. I know her well and recommend her highly. Shall we see if she has some time free?"

- Be a resource and referral guide. Most clients are familiar with the process of being referred to a specialist; it happens in human medicine all the time. You might say something like, "Paul, if you had a broken arm, you wouldn't walk around for three weeks without having it looked at. The same is true with a broken heart. I know someone who can help you with the process of healing from both Janie and Betsy's deaths. Let's call him now and see if he can set up an appointment to see you today or tomorrow."

- Educate with a back-door approach. This is usually a less threatening method for clients since they do not perceive it as being aimed directly at them. Many adults will seek help for their children or for another member of their family even if they are reluctant to ask for help for themselves. You might say something like, "Joan, I know you and Paul have other children. Have you thought about how you might help them cope with the connection between Janie and Betsy's deaths? There are some very effective ways to help children deal with loss, and I work with a woman who can provide you with this information. Would you like to have her name and number?"

Situation 15
Suicidal Clients

Client: *"Life means nothing to me without Pepper.*
          Sometimes I wonder why I should go on ..."

What's Going on Here?

A remark like this is usually a normal reaction to loss. It's called sui-cide ideation and is simply an indication of the griever's deep feelings of despair. For many pet owners, it is difficult to imagine what their daily routines will be like without their pets. Losing such significant relationships can feel overwhelming.

On rare occasions, though, there may be suicidal intent underlying the client's comment. This may mean that a client may seriously consider suicide when their companion animal dies.

Therefore, it's important for you to know how to determine the differ-ence between a normal grief reaction and a suicidal one. You also need to know how to help in the latter situation.

How Can I Help?

Suicidal people usually are not mentally ill. Rather, they have become so distraught that they think they have a very narrowed range of op-tions or choices in life. Ultimately, they are unable to see any other so-lution to their problems but to end their own lives. Most people who attempt suicide are ambivalent about the act. They don't really want to kill themselves; they just want to find an end to their overwhelming feelings of distress.

There is a common myth about suicide that says if you ask people di-rectly about their suicidal comments, you'll somehow condone the act and encourage them to kill themselves. Yet, the opposite is actually true. Open, honest discussions about suicide can lower a person's anxi-ety level and actually make the event less likely to occur.

Attending to suicidal comments can make people feel supported and more understood. To attend to clients who demonstrate suicidal intent, you should ask specific questions about how your clients feel and why they would want to die. Also, you should not use euphemisms like pass away or cross over about death. Euphemisms indicate anxiety with the subject matter at hand. If you are too anxious to talk about suicide, you won't be able to help your client deal realistically with feelings.

How aggressive you need to be in seeing that a potentially suicidal client receives help depends partially on what is called the lethality of the situation. To assess lethality, you need to:

1. Determine whether or not your client has a specific plan and how quickly he or she could put a plan into action. For instance, has your client collected medication and determined the dosage that would be fatal? Does your client now have the bottle of pills in hand, or would the client have to first obtain a prescription and then go to the drugstore to pick them up?

2. Assess if the method your client has chosen has a high probability of quick success. For example, slashing wrists versus using a hand gun.

3. Ascertain whether or not your client is isolated and alone or is in close proximity to someone who can help.

If suicidal clients are not in immediate danger, encourage them to call a crisis or suicide hotline, a friend or relative, their family physician, a member of the clergy, or a therapist, if they have one. You may also choose to call one of these individuals yourself on their behalf. If you decide you must notify someone, always tell your client. Explain that, if they are unwilling to make the call themselves, you will make the call for them. If you say this in a firm, supportive way, rather than in a scolding or threatening manner, most clients will agree to call someone themselves.

Keep in Mind

- There are no clear patterns that predict suicide, but there are age and gender differences among those who do take their own lives. For instance, men commit suicide more often than women, and elderly people have the highest suicide rates. Suicide is also a leading cause of death among older adolescents, college students, and young adults under age 25.

- When providing client support, some people attempt to make contracts with suicidal clients, insisting a client agree to call them before they carry through with a suicide plan. This is not a good idea for veterinary professionals. If a client calls you when the lethality of the situation is high, you may quickly be in over your head in terms of your training and capabilities. In addition, if you receive a call from a suicidal client, you may also be tempted to go to them in order to try to prevent his or her death. However, you should never go to a client's house or attempt to rescue them, no matter where they may be. There is always the potential for suicidal clients to turn homicidal, and your own life could be in danger if you attempt any kind of direct help.

Quick Tips

What to Say, What to Do

- Acknowledge every comment containing suicide ideation and take it seriously. Paraphrase what your client has just said, perhaps by saying, "It sounds like you can't imagine life without Pepper."

- Next, be direct and ask the tough questions. Too many questions can make you sound nervous or like an interrogator. Simply ask your client, "Are you thinking of taking your own life now that Pepper has died?"

  Most often your client will say (perhaps with some embarrassment or anger), "No, of course not. I'm just so upset—I didn't want to lose him." In this case, you can relax and be quite sure that your client's comment represents a normal grief reaction. You might say, "I'm glad to hear that. We take these comments very seriously here, and I always feel it is my responsibility to ask people what they mean when they say them."

  However, if the answer is, "Yes, I've thought about it occasionally. She's all I have … ," you need to 1) assess the lethality of your client's situation (See How Can I Help?), 2) support your client through the immediate crisis and, 3) refer your client to an appropriate human service agency or professional, or contact the appropriate resource yourself. In other words, practice facilitating and being a referral resource.

- All too often, when people least expect it, suicidal people take their own lives. In depressed states, people may want to kill themselves but simply can't find the energy to plan and carry through with it. As the most severe symptoms of depression lift, though, the ability to think more clearly and to act more forcefully returns, and suicide often becomes a reality.

- Occasionally, a client who is preparing for suicide may bring a pet in for euthanasia so the pet will not be left without care. It's very important to ask why a client is requesting that the companion animal be euthanized, especially if the animal is healthy.

- Although thoughts and comments about suicide are quite common, truly suicidal clients are very rare. The odds are high that you will never encounter one. If you do, you should talk with a trained human service professional who can advise you about what actions to take and about who can also support you. Being involved in someone's attempted or completed suicide can be emotionally devastating for you. If it happens, you need to take care of yourself and talk to someone about it. No one can assume responsibility for someone else's life. You will need to be reassured that you were not responsible, either directly or indirectly, for your client's decision to end his or her life.

How Will I Know if I've Been Successful?

When providing client support, the main strategy for suicide intervention is to stop any self-destructive behavior that might take place during the crisis time when your client feels total despair. In most cases, suicidal intent is present for only a short time. Soon after, most gain control, make a new and, healthier plan, and go on.

The best strategy you can use if you encounter a truly suicidal client is to get help. In most communities, professional help is not hard to find. There are suicide or crisis intervention centers staffed with well-trained people you can call for advice or debriefing. In addition, most mental health agencies have a professional on staff who is authorized to hospitalize people on a short-term basis for observation and for their own protection. Many hospitals offer this service, too.

Finally, the most effective and immediate help you can get is the police. The rule of thumb regarding whether or not to contact law enforcement authorities is to do so whenever someone makes a serious threat to do harm to self or others. This is the code police officers use as a guide for intervening in potentially dangerous situations. When they learn that you are concerned about a potential suicide, the police will do what is called a welfare check. This means they will locate your client and either intervene to prevent a suicide that is taking place or make sure the danger of suicide is not imminent.

Figure 7
Keys to Making Referrals

Several variables can help you predict which of your clients may have more intense grief responses when their companion animals die and thus require more of your time. These red flags may also alert you to which clients may benefit from referrals to one or more human service professionals for further counseling and ongoing support.

- Cases that involve children
- Ceremonial owner-present euthanasias
- Clients who anthropomorphize (assign human characteristics) their pets to an unrealistic level
- Clients who have invested significant amounts of time, energy, and money in their companion animals' treatment
- Clients who have recently experienced other significant losses and/or stressors (e.g., death of a family member, major illness, divorce, loss of a job, recent move, birth of a child)
- Clients who identify their companion animals as their children, best friends, or primary source of support
- Clients who live alone and cannot identify other sources of emotional support
- Clients who may be clinically depressed or those who make references to suicide, homicide, abuse, or violence
- Clients who symbolically link their pets to another person, relationship, or time in their lives. Symbolic links often develop from previous losses and grief that is still unresolved.

Figure 8
National Pet Loss Hot lines

The majority of these hot lines are staffed by volunteers (veterinary students and veterinary professionals) who have received some paraprofessional training in helping pet owners deal with pet loss.

916/752-4200—University of California at Davis
Weekdays 6:30 p.m. to 9:30 p.m. PT

352/392-4700 x 4080—University of Florida
Weekdays 7 p.m. to 9 p.m. ET

517/432-2696—Michigan State College of Veterinary Medicine
Tuesday to Thursday, 6:30 p.m. to 9:30 p.m. ET

630/603-3994—Chicago VMA
Leave voice-mail message. Calls will be returned 7 p.m. to 9 p.m. CT. Long-distance calls will be returned collect.

540/231-8038—Virginia-Maryland Regional College of Veterinary Medicine
Tuesday and Thursday, 6 p.m. to 9 p.m. ET

614/292-1823—Ohio State University
Monday, Wednesday, and Friday, 6:30 p.m. to 9:30 p.m. ET. Voice-mail messages will be returned collect during operating hours.

508/839-7966—Tufts University School of Veterinary Medicine
Weekdays, 6 p.m. to 9 p.m. ET. Voice-mail messages will be returned daily, collect outside Massachusetts.

Client Support Resources

Tools For You to Use

Referral Network

Resource	Contact	Telephone Number

Pet Loss

Local pet loss counselor

Local pet loss support group

Medical Referrals

Veterinary medical specialists

Specialty

Specialty

Specialty

Nearest veterinary medical
teaching hospital/research center

Animal Behavior

Certified animal behaviorist

Obedience trainer

Other Human Services

Animal abuse

Child/spouse abuse

Clergy

Crisis hotline

Suicide prevention

Substance abuse

**Emergency numbers for your local police,
ambulance, and fire departments**

Know your resources! Update this list often. Make multiple copies
and post them by each telephone. Write addresses and the names of
specific contact people on the back. Obtain business cards from your
resource and referral network contacts and make them available to
your clients.

Client Support Feedback

Three Praises and a Wish

On a scale of 1 to 5, with 5 being outstanding, rate your own or your colleague's performance in each area appropriate to an act of providing client support. Include specific ideas regarding what you or your colleague did well and what needs to be improved. Discuss results at staff meetings.

Performance Area	Rating *(1=poor 2 3 4 5=outstanding)*
Client Support Roles	
Being a resource and referral guide	_____
Being a source of support	_____
Educating	_____
Facilitating	_____
Client Support Techniques	
Acknowledging	_____
Active listening	_____
Asking tough questions	_____
Attending	_____
Giving permission	_____
Normalizing	_____
Paraphrasing	_____
Responding with touch	_____
Self-disclosing	_____
Structuring the environment	_____
Using minimal encouragers	_____
Using necessary silences	_____

Three Praises

You performed especially well in these three areas. I was impressed!

_____

_____

_____

A Wish

You could improve in this area. Keep practicing!

_____

_____

_____

References

1. Fogle, B., and D. Abrahamson. 1990. Pet loss: a survey of the attitudes and feelings of practicing veterinarians. *Anthrozoos* 3 (3):143–150.

2. McKey, E., and K. Payne. 1992. APPMA study: pet ownership soars. *Pet Business* 18 (8):22–23.

3. American Pet Products Manufacturers Association. 1988. Survey of pet ownership in the USA. *Pet Business* 14 (8).

4. Friedmann, E., A. H. Katcher, J. J. Lynch, and S. A. Thomas. 1982. Animal companions and one-year survival of patients after discharge from a coronary care unit. *California Veterinarian* 8:45–50.

5. ———. 1980. Animal companions and one-year survival of patients after discharge from a coronary care unit. *Public Health Report* 95 (4):307–312.

6. Hart, L. A., B. L. Hart, and B. Mader. 1990. Humane euthanasia and companion animal death: caring for the animal, the client, and the veterinarian. *JAVMA* 197 (10):1292–1299.

7. Gage, G., and R. Holcomb. 1991. Couples' perceptions of the stressfulness of the death of the family pet. *Family Relations* 40 (1).

8. Hart, L. A., and B. L. Hart. 1987. Grief and stress from so many animal deaths. *Companion Animal Practice* 1(1):20–21.

9. Harris, J. A study of client responses to death or loss in a companion animal veterinary practice. In Katcher, A. H., and A. M. Beck, eds. 1983. *New perspectives on our lives with companion animals*. Philadelphia: Univ. of Pennsylvania Press. 370–376.

10. Loss: An interview with University of Chicago's Froma Walsh. 1992. *Psychology Today* 25 (4):64–94.

11. Frey, W. H., with M. Lanseth. 1985. *Crying: the mystery of tears*. Minneapolis: Winston Press.

12. Ibid.

13. Peters, R. 1987. *Practical intelligence*. New York: Harper and Row. 96.

14. Antelyes, J. 1990. Client hopes, client expectations. *JAVMA* 197 (12):1596–1597.

15. Troutman, C. M. 1988. *The veterinary services market for companion animals*. Overland Park, Kansas: Charles, Charles, Research Group and Schaumburg, Illinois: the American Veterinary Medical Association.

16. Good communication keeps clients coming back. 1989. *DVM Management Consultants Reports* 20 (5):1.

17. Fudin, C. E. Basic skills for successful client relations. In Cohen, S. P., and C. E. Fudin, eds. *Problems in veterinary medicine: animal illness and human emotion*. 3 (1):7–20.

18. Mehrabian, A. 1968. Communication without words. *Psychology Today* (September): 53.

Resources

Support-based Referral Services

The Delta Society
289 Perimeter Road East
Renton, Washington 98055
206/226-7357
Delta can supply a Pet Loss and Bereavement Packet, a Directory of Pet Loss Resources, and/or a Pet Loss Packet Supplement for veterinary or mental health professionals. The Directory includes a state-by-state listing of local pet loss counselors and support groups as well as descriptions of services offered by various university-based pet loss programs across the country.

Changes: The Support for People and Pets Program
Colorado State University Veterinary Teaching Hospital
300 West Drake
Fort Collins, Colorado 80523
970/491-1242
Changes can supply grief education materials and individual grief support.

Pet Loss Support Hotline
University of California-Davis
Bonnie Mader, MS, Director
Weekdays, 6:30–9:30 p.m. Pacific time
916/752-4200
Staffed by veterinary student volunteers; telephone counseling at the pet owner's expense.

Video and Audio Tapes About Pet Loss

Pet Loss and Bereavement Series
This videotape series will help your staff recognize the characteristics of grief and foster client understanding of bereavement. The first two videotapes, *Understanding Client Pet Loss* and *Counseling Clients*, include one companion workbook each. The third tape, *The Loss of Your Pet*, includes ten client booklets.
American Animal Hospital Association
Phone: 800/252-2242 or 303/986-2800
Fax: 303/986-1700

Friends for Life: Loving and Losing Your Animal Companion (audiotape)
Sounds True Audio
PO Box 8010
Boulder, Colorado 80306-8010
Phone: 800/333-9185
Fax: 303/665-5292

Pamphlets

The Loss of Your Pet
American Animal Hospital Association
Phone: 800/252-2242 or 303/986-2800
Fax: 303/986-1700

Pet Loss and Human Emotion: When the Question is Euthanasia
AVMA
1931 North Meacham Road, Suite 100
Schaumburg, Illinois 60173-4360
800/248-AVMA

Books About Pet Loss for Adults

Church, J. A. *Joy in a Woolly Coat: Living With, Loving, & Letting Go of Treasured Animal Friends*. H. J. Kramer Inc., 1987.

Nieberg, H. A., and A. Fisher. *Pet Loss: A Thoughtful Guide for Adults and Children*. Harper & Row, 1982.

Montgomery, M., and H. Montgomery. *A Final Act of Caring: Ending the Life of an Animal Friend*. Montgomery Press, 1993. (Available from AAHA)

———. *Goodbye, My Friend: Grieving the Loss of a Pet*. Montgomery Press, 1991. (Available from AAHA)

Quackenbush, J., and D. Graveline. *When Your Pet Dies: How to Cope With Your Feelings*. Simon & Schuster, 1985. (Available from AAHA)

Books About Pet Loss for Children (and Parents)

Carrick, C. *The Accident*. Clarion Books, 1981.

Morehead, D. *A Special Place for Charlee: A Child's Companion Through Pet Loss*. Partners in Publishing, 1996. (Available from AAHA)

Rogers, F. *When a Pet Dies*. Putnam Publishing Group, 1988.

Sibbitt, S. *Oh, Where Has My Pet Gone?* B. Libby Press, 1991.

Varley, S. *Badger's Parting Gifts*. Lothrop, Lee, & Shepard Books, 1984.

Viorst, J. *The Tenth Good Thing About Barney*. Atheneum, 1971. (Available from AAHA)

Wilhelm, H. *I'll Always Love You*. Crown Publishing Group, 1985.

Books About Loss and Grief—Self-help

There are dozens of books about loss and grief. Many address specific losses like the death of a mother, father, child, sibling, or companion animal. Some of the more well-known books are listed here. Check with your library or bookstore for other books appropriate to your needs.

Colgrove, M., H. H. Bloomfield, and P. McWilliams. *How to Survive the Loss of a Love*. Prelude Press, 1991.

James, J., and F. Cherry. *The Grief Recovery Handbook*. Harper & Row, 1988.

Levine, S. *Healing Into Life and Death*. Anchor Books/Double Day, 1987.

Linn, E. *I Know Just how You Feel … Avoiding the Clichés of Grief*. The Publishers Mark, 1986.

Rando, T. A. *How to Go on Living When Someone You Love Dies*. Bantam, 1991.

Staudacher, C. *Beyond Grief: A Guide for Recovering From the Death of a Loved One*. New Harbinger Publishers, 1987.

———. *Men and Grief: A Guide for Men Surviving the Death of a Loved One*. New Harbinger Publishers, 1991.

Tatelbaum, J. *The Courage to Grieve*. Harper & Row, 1980.

———. *You Don't Have to Suffer: A Handbook for Moving Beyond Life's Crises*. Harper & Row, 1989.

Books about Loss and Grief for Young Children (and Parents)

Grollman, E. *Talking About Death: A Dialogue Between Parents and Children*. Putnam/Beacon Press, 1990.

Jewett, C. L. *Helping Children Cope With Separation and Loss*. The Harvard Common Press, 1982.

Stein, S. B. *About Dying: An Open Family Book for Parents and Children Together*. Walker & Company, 1984.

Grief Theory, Counseling, and Therapy

Cook, A. S., and D. Dworkin. *Helping the Bereaved: Therapeutic Interventions for Children, Adolescents, and Adults*. Basic Books, 1992.

Kubler-Ross, E. *On Death and Dying*. Collier Books/MacMillan Publishing Company, 1969.

Lagoni, L., C. Butler, and S. Hetts. *The Human-Animal Bond and Grief*. W.B. Saunders Company, 1994.

Rando, T. A. *Grief, Dying, and Death: Clinical Interventions for Caregivers*. Research Press Company, 1984.

Glossary

acknowledging. To recognize the existence or truth of something.

active listening. To listen for feelings, rather than the factual content of conversations.

anticipatory grief. The grief that occurs prior to an actual loss or death. Examples of pet loss situations that may trigger anticipatory grief include aging pets and pets who are terminally ill. The symptoms of anticipatory grief include any or all of the symptoms of normal grief.

attending. Body language which lets the person who is talking know that careful attention is being paid to what is being said.

complicated grief. The circumstances surrounding a pet's death which make grieving more difficult than usual. Examples of factors that often complicate grief for pet owners are feelings of responsibility for a pet's accidental death, feelings of guilt after deciding to euthanize a pet, and the general tendency for society to trivialize companion animal death.

euthanasia, ceremonial client-present. A medical procedure during which pet owners witness the humane termination of an animal's life. During the procedure, pet owners' needs and grief responses are attended to in a sensitive and compassionate manner. The use of ritual, ceremony, and effective helping strategies are encouraged in order to promote positive grief outcomes for survivors.

giving permission. Encouraging clients to think, feel, and behave however they need to, within safe limits, without fear of judgment.

grief. The normal way to adjust to endings and changes. Grief is a necessary process for healing emotional wounds.

helping. Providing short-term assistance, mainly information and comfort, to others before, during, and shortly following a death.

human-animal bond. A popular way of referring to the types of relationships and attachments people form with animals, particularly companion animals. Also, an accepted area of scholarly research.

loss. An ending or a point of change or transition. Loss can be permanent, as in death, or temporary, as in the loss of a job.

normalizing. Lending credibility to others' thoughts, feelings, behaviors, and experiences.

primary loss. The actual loss of something or someone and the main cause of grief. An example in terms of pet loss is the actual death of a companion animal.

secondary loss. Disruptions and changes in peoples' lives due to a primary loss. An example in terms of pet loss is the loss of routine and shared activity such as walks or participation in competitive shows that occurs when companion animals die.

self-disclosure. Briefly sharing a personal experience when it may be appropriate and of use to someone else.

structuring the environment. Adapting the physical elements of an environment to better meet the situation at hand.

surrogate grief. Grief that belongs to one person (e.g., a pet owner) but is experienced or carried by someone else (e.g., a shelter worker or a veterinary professional) due to the owner's absence, indifference, or inability to grieve.

symbolic loss. A loss that is associated with a previous loss in life. An example in terms of pet loss is the loss of a pet who links a pet owner to a special person, place, thing, or time in life (e.g., a spouse who has died, a marriage that has ended). The pet's death ends the link. Although pet loss is significant in its own right, the grief owners feel due to a symbolic loss is often more intense.

touch. Providing comfort and demonstrating care and concern by use of physical contact.

unresolved grief. Occurs when normal grief is prevented free expression or when, for some reason, the normal grief process is arrested or blocked. Unresolved or unfinished issues due to an earlier, significant loss are frequently re-stimulated during pet loss. Many pet owners struggle with the impact of a past loss during their experiences with pet loss.

Meet the Author

Laurel Lagoni and Willie

Laurel Lagoni earned a master's degree in Human Development and Family Studies from Colorado State University in 1984. She co-founded and co-directed Changes: The Support for People and Pets Program at the Colorado State University Veterinary Teaching Hospital. The Changes program provides pet owners with grief education and support during emergencies, diagnoses, treatment procedures, decision-making, unexpected deaths, euthanasias, and bereavement follow-up. As a veterinary grief counselor with the Changes program, Ms. Lagoni worked for 10 years alongside veterinarians and animal health technicians as a member of the case management teams and facilitated the emotional aspects of hundreds of the teaching hospital's medical cases.

As an instructor in the professional veterinary medical curriculum, Ms. Lagoni developed a comprehensive curriculum and taught thousands of students and veterinary professionals about the human-animal bond, effective communication and client relations techniques, veterinary grief counseling, and client-present euthanasia. She also co-authored the textbook *The Human-Animal Bond and Grief* with Carolyn Butler, MS, and Suzanne Hetts, PhD, and was a consultant to AAHA during the development of its *Pet Loss and Bereavement* videotape training series.